Redemption Song

Also by Louis Rapoport

THE LOST JEWS: LAST OF THE ETHIOPIAN FALASHAS

Redemption Song

The Story of Operation Moses

Louis Rapoport

HARCOURT BRACE JOVANOVICH, PUBLISHERS

San Diego   New York   London

*Requests for permission to make copies of any
part of the work should be mailed to:
Permissions, Harcourt Brace Jovanovich, Publishers,
Orlando, Florida 32887.*

Library of Congress Cataloging in Publication Data

Rapoport, Louis.
Redemption song.
Bibliography: p.
Includes index.
1. Falasha Rescue, 1984–1985.   2. Israel—Emigration
and immigration.   3. Falashas—Israel.   4. Ethiopia—
Ethnic relations.   5. Israel—Ethnic relations.
I. Title.   II. Title: Operation Moses.
DS135.E75R28 1986   362.8'7'089924063   85-30489
ISBN 0-15-176120-5

*Printed in the United States of America
First edition*
A B C D E

To those who saved thousands, and to the memory of those who died along the way

Contents

Eight pages of photographs follow page 110.

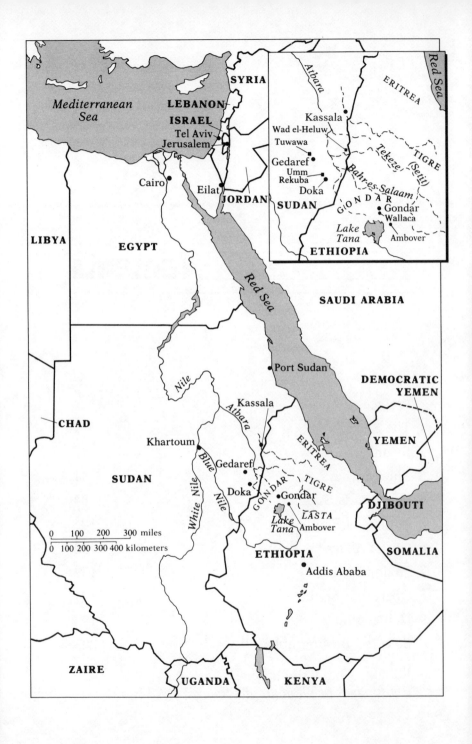

Preface

The airlift that brought some eight thousand Ethiopian Jewish refugees from Sudan to Israel beginning in November 1984 ignited the imagination of headline writers around the world: "Rescue of the Lost Tribe," "Bravo Israel!" "Exodus of the Black Jews," and "Hallelujah!" *New York Times* columnist William Safire declared that the reason for Israel's existence had been reaffirmed: "For the first time in history, thousands of black people are being brought into a country not

in chains but in dignity, not as slaves but as citizens.
. . . Israel's quiet acceptance of responsibility should
say a great deal to Africa, to American blacks and
Jews and to all who believe that the 'Falashas' of the
world should be strangers no more." *The Times* of
London said that the airlift was "in its way as inspiring a story as the Biblical Exodus." It was a dramatic chapter in Jewish and Israeli history—and with
its biblical resonances, it held universal appeal.

What came to be known as Operation Moses is a
complex story about an ancient people who felt
themselves driven "home" to the Holy Land. The
Mossad, Israel's secret service, did the most to bring
the Falashas to Israel, and details of that effort are
presented here for the first time. But there would not
have been an Operation Moses without the active
participation of the United States. The State Department's key role in initiating the airlift is also revealed in this book for the first time.

There is a dark side to the story as well: a UN
agency was guilty of covering up the deaths of thousands of Ethiopian Jewish refugees in the camps of
eastern Sudan in the summer of 1984; some of the
Falasha leaders in the camps withheld vital aid from
their suffering people; negligent politicians and would-
be deliverers sometimes harmed the cause they
claimed to be struggling for. But for the most part,
Operation Moses restates Israel's dedication to the
preservation of the Jewish people and to the principle that never again will any threatened Jewish community be abandoned to its fate.

Nine years before Operation Moses, in December
1975 (shortly after the Marxist takeover), I sat on top
of a jungly hill in Ethiopia with a group of armed

young blacks who told me that some day they would
be reunited with their brethren in Israel. One of the
young Jews, clad in a white Ethiopian toga and
clutching an ancient rifle, looked particularly fierce
when he said that nothing would stop them—not the
armies clashing in northern Ethiopia a year after
Haile Selassie's overthrow, not the swarms of bandits that regularly pillage Ethiopian villages, not the
poverty and periodic famine and disease, and not the
handful of recalcitrant Israeli officials who still opposed the Jerusalem government's ruling of that year
which recognized the Falashas as Jews, eligible to
become Israelis. He said that his people, who called
themselves Beta-Israel (the House of Israel), would be
"redeemed." Although I was already a believer in their
cause, it all seemed a bit surreal. It was still difficult
for me to think of these tribesmen in the remote
highlands of northwestern Ethiopia as fellow Jews.
But it was I, not my fierce-looking friend, who was
lacking in understanding of Jewish identity.

IT GOES AGAINST my journalistic grain to intrude my-
self into a story I'm covering. But I believe in this case
that something has to be said about how I got to the
story and how it got to me. Much of the book is written from the perspective of an Ethiopian Jew I call
Yehuda, based on a man who took part in crucial aspects of the rescue of thousands of his people. It is
their story, not mine. But I believe that the personal
note may be helpful in understanding some of the
reasons it took so long for the Jews of the world to
recognize the Falashas (the word means "stranger,"
"wanderer," or "exile" in Ge'ez [Ethiopic], the liturgical language of Christian and Jewish Ethiopians

alike) as their coreligionists, entitled to immigrate to Israel under the Law of Return. American Jews, who were galvanized into involvement on behalf of the Falashas in 1984–85 and raised over $50 million for their integration into Israeli society, have had to overcome a great many barriers dividing them from the black Jews. And this was also true for several Israeli leaders who came from an Eastern European background, like most of their American-Jewish brethren.

I have been an Israeli for twelve years and my children's first language is Hebrew, but when I was growing up in California, I was far removed from Israel and the Jewish world and never knew that I was part of such a varied mosaic. American Jews simply never conceived of the possibility that there was an entire community of black Jews, whose roots went back thousands of years. Jews were all from Poland or Russia. Who ever heard of a Jew from Morocco or from India? That was pure esoterica; and a black Jew living in a thatched conical hut in the African bush was beyond belief.

Many American Jews who come to Israel for the first time are struck by their discovery that "the policemen are Jewish," that "the supermarkets are Jewish," that there are dumb Jewish punks and Jewish hookers and low-life criminals as well as the expected professors and scientists and soldier-farmers. And it is not always easy for the visiting American Jew to accept the fact that "his" Israel is composed of a majority of Jews who are from Asian and North African countries, that the darker, more "primitive" Jews outnumber the Ashkenazim from Eastern Europe, South America, and the Anglophone countries.

American Jews and many Israeli Jews had a similar initial reaction to the fact that there were black Jews from the mountains of Africa and that they wanted to come to Israel—"What next?"

Although I'm still not sure why I started to write about the black Jews of Ethiopia in 1974, I think it did have to do with finding my own place in a multifarious Israel. I felt—and still feel—remote from the Jewish religion, but I was greatly moved by the liturgical works of the Beta-Israel, which I read in Wolf Leslau's *Falasha Anthology*, first published in 1951. I too believed in the God of Israel, paradise and hell, angels, the Redemption and the Messiah, the Resurrection and the Last Judgment. I too felt cut off from Hebrew and the rabbinical tradition, albeit for entirely different reasons.

In 1974 when I presented the editors of the *Jerusalem Post* with a five-thousand-word article about the persecution of the Falashas in Ethiopia and Israel's unwillingness to recognize or help the Ethiopian Jews, I got the third degree. "Who put you up to this?" I was asked. I said it seemed that an injustice was being done, that in the light of Zionist propaganda about the Ingathering of the Exiles, something ought to be done about the most ancient Jewish community in the Diaspora, the only community that wished to immigrate to Israel *en masse*. The article was a solid and honest account, based on dozens of interviews, and the editors could not bring themselves to kill it. I would like to think that it had some effect—especially since it appeared simultaneously in *Ha'aretz*, the country's leading newspaper—and that thereafter, at least one skeleton was out of the Zionist closet. But in fact, my articles and first book, *The Lost Jews* (1980),

had little impact. Menachem Begin, who started up
the machinery for the rescue of the Ethiopian Jews in
1977 and then again in 1980, didn't read my book
until Operation Moses was over.

   Begin was perhaps the only Israeli leader of recent
years to identify closely with the Ethiopian Jews.
When Israel was established in 1948, the leaders of
the new nation were Eastern European Ashkenazim.
One of their first priorities was to bring the stateless
survivors of the Holocaust to the renascent Jewish
homeland. Waves of emigrants from other lands—
principally the Arab countries of Africa and the Near
East—would soon follow. But in the era of David Ben-
Gurion and Chaim Weizmann, few knew or cared
about the Jews of black Africa. The exception was
Yitzhak Ben-Zvi, Israel's second president, a scholar
who had become an expert on the supposed whereabouts of the Ten Lost Tribes of Israel. The rule was
Yosef Burg, the National Religious party boss who has
served in every Israeli cabinet since 1951 and who was
hostile to the Beta-Israel from the outset. Though he
had gone to school with a Falasha in a Jewish institution in Germany in the late 1920s and early 1930s,
Burg thought these people could not possibly be Jews.
He once told me, "You might as well write a book
about the Martians."

   In the politics of immigration, Israeli leaders quite
naturally tried to attract the most educated Jews. For
decades, nothing at all was spent on helping the
Ethiopian Jews, who were among the poorest people
in one of the poorest countries on earth. Jerusalem's
relations with Haile Selassie's Ethiopia were considered to be the bedrock of Israel's Africa policy, and
in the 1960s and early 1970s, Israel was officially "not

enthusiastic" about encouraging the Falashas to emigrate. As former foreign minister Abba Eban once
told me, the Ethiopian Jews were "a marginal problem," and in the many years he served in the cabinet, the subject was "never brought up." Golda Meir
had once reportedly said of the Falashas, "Don't we
have enough problems?" Nor did the rabbinical establishment move to rule on whether the Falashas
were Jews. There was a long and bitter fight by the
Falashas and their friends to change the perception
that the Ethiopian Jews didn't really matter. But the
change occurred. People who once had arrogantly
dismissed the idea that the Falashas were Jews later
came into contact with them and were duly "converted," as I had been; and they dedicated themselves to saving the Beta-Israel from extinction.

In the first half of the 1980s, famine and pestilence
threatened millions of people in northeast Africa. The
Falashas, too, were imperiled by starvation and a host
of diseases. Up to three thousand died, but about fifteen thousand were saved. For many, Operation Moses
made the difference.

MOST OF THIS book was written during stays in the
United States and was therefore not liable to Israeli
censorship provisions. However, I have felt obliged to
withhold many details of Israeli operations in the
Horn of Africa because lives still are at risk—several
innocent people who were thought to have helped Israeli agents are being held in the horrible prisons of
Ethiopia and Sudan. And eight to ten thousand more
Ethiopian Jews are waiting to leave Africa in order
to rejoin their families. This is why top Israeli officials such as Shimon Peres and Yitzhak Shamir, as

xviPREFACE

well as former prime minister Menachem Begin, have
kept completely mum on the subject. But many details of the operation have emerged.

My reconstruction of certain scenes that took place
during Operation Moses is based on information I
obtained from U.S. and Israeli officials, operatives,
and other sources. Though I believe my version is the
most informed and accurate one available, the full
story will probably not be known for years because
of the ongoing questions of security.

Special thanks go to my Ethiopian sources, who
must remain anonymous. Names and some details
have been altered to protect that anonymity. Much
of the information about "Yehuda" has been gleaned
from his friends, relatives, and fellow workers—Yehuda himself was basically closemouthed. This reluctance to talk was also true of "Aleph," the Israeli
Falasha who was sent to Sudan for Operation Moses.

I wish to thank historian Steven Kaplan of the Ben-
Zvi Institute in Jerusalem for helping me chronicle Beta-Israel history in the Ethiopian context. Dr.
Kaplan is one of a growing number of Israeli experts
on various aspects of Ethiopian and Beta-Israel studies, and several of them are cited in *Redemption Song*.

I am grateful to the leadership of the United Jewish Appeal in the United States for granting me the
exclusive right to cover the Operation Moses fund-
raising campaign and to detail for the first time the
UJA's workings in an emergency situation. My thanks
also to Joel Rebibo for his assistance on a section of
the chapter concerning absorption. My wife, Sylvia,
provided me with constant support and encourage-
ment while managing a busy household. My agent,
Helen Rees, and my editor, John Radziewicz, have

been enthusiastic and encouraging throughout this project. I am most grateful to *Jerusalem Post* editors Erwin Frenkel and Ari Rath for sending me to Sudan, the United States, and Europe to cover various aspects of Operation Moses.

The title of the book comes from a reggae song by the late Bob Marley, a member of the Rastafarian sect, which believed that Emperor Haile Selassie of Ethiopia was God on earth. Although that belief seems to me rather wide of the mark, the song captures something of the universalistic wish for deliverance—which ultimately is what Operation Moses is all about.

September 1985

1

The Shepherd

When Israel came
into existence in 1948, ten-year-old Yehuda was a
shepherd in the Ethiopian highlands near copper-
tinted Lake Tana, source of the Nile's headwaters. The
news, which reached his village weeks after independence was declared, awakened great expectations
among his poverty-ridden people, the Jews of Ethiopia known as Falashas. Some of the religious leaders
of Ambover village said that the lightning of redemption had struck and that their exile in Ethiopia,

1

which had lasted for over two thousand years, would soon end. Others, including Yehuda's grandfather, disagreed vehemently and said that they were the generation of the desert, that forty years would pass before the Falashas would enter the Holy Land.

But Yehuda's grandfather, and the elders of that generation, were all agreed on the basic message that the turbaned priests and deacons preached every day in the mud-wattle houses and synagogues of some five hundred Falasha villages: "The time will come when we will return to Zion by the route which brought us to Ethiopia—from the west we came, and we are destined to return by the same route."

At the time, the words didn't mean very much to Yehuda, a stubborn, strong-willed boy who lived in a one-room round *tukul* with his parents and eleven sisters and brothers. Although Yehuda was in awe of his priestly grandfather and respected the sage for his inspiring sermons, he cared mainly about his animals, the cattle that he tended. Nevertheless, the religion of his people, an ancient form of Judaism, was never remote from him. Yehuda's relatives included an important priest of the Falashas and a young man who would eventually become the first Ethiopian Jewish rabbi.

Wealth in Africa is measured by grain and livestock, and Yehuda's family was relatively well-off, even though they had to pay the absentee nobleman who owned their land over 70 percent of the annual crop of peanuts, vegetables, and *teff*, a grain grown only in Ethiopia. Although they lived with their chickens in a single room with a dirt floor, they had the second biggest herd of livestock in the village and never wanted for food, even during the area's periodic famines. The intense, hawk-nosed Yehuda was in charge of the family's living wealth. He had given every cow and goat a name, and he took his responsibilities very seriously.

One day his two older sisters, whose job was to prepare meals for the large family, refused to make him his lunch and bring it out to the fields; they teased him, saying that he didn't know how to take proper care of the herd. Yehuda plotted revenge.

One of the girls' chores was to bring water to the hut every evening. Going out in the dark was a terrifying experience in Ethiopia, where there was a constant fear of *shiftas*—the bandits who roam the countryside on horseback—and the myriad demons that haunt the Ethiopians. (The Falashas, like their Christian and Moslem neighbors in the highlands, were besieged by superstition.)

Yehuda's father had rigged up a gravity-fed water supply, piping the water to a location very near the family's hut, but still the girls had to walk about a hundred yards to the tap. One night soon after his sisters had teased him, Yehuda took off all his clothes, rubbed coal over his entire body, and sat on a big rock waiting for them. When the girls passed in the dark, carrying their pails slung over their shoulders, he smiled broadly, and his teeth flashed eerily in the moonlight. "It's the Devil!" screamed Aloumash, the eldest of the sisters. The pails crashed to the ground. Yehuda's mother rushed from the hut and fainted when she saw the demonical apparition. Yehuda, mortified by what he had done, ran away from home—and his family then realized who the demon was.

But when he came back the next day, all was forgiven. His father ruled that Yehuda had been pro-voked, and he went back to tending the flock. His sisters no longer refused to make his lunch and stopped teasing him. At an early age, the shepherd boy had gained a particular kind of respect from members of his family.

Yehuda dreamed one night that a gray-haired "big man" he didn't know came to him as he stood next to a tree, watching over his flock. The important-looking personage threw him a long white string to tie up a black calf, and later a cow and a steer and several other calves. Then Yehuda thanked the man.

Yehuda told his dream to his grandfather, who took him to the hut of a woman who interpreted dreams. She said that it meant Yehuda would go to Israel while still a youth. The long white string represented two things: their people's ancient hopes to return to the land of Israel, and the long days he would be away. The cow and the steer and the other calves represented the rest of his family—they too would reach the Holy Land one day, with the help of Ye-huda. The interpreter suggested that the gray-haired man might be Yona Bogala, the distinguished teacher and scholar who represented his people's interests in Addis Ababa and who funneled the small amount of aid sent to the Ethiopian Jews by a handful of En-glish and American Jews.

Ambover was the biggest Falasha village, with about three hundred thatch-roofed *tukuls*, a pan-roofed synagogue, and the main school, which drew Ethio-pian Jews from all over the Gondar region. But the school went up to only the sixth grade. In order to continue his education, Yehuda had to leave the vil-lage where the Jews lived isolated from their gentile neighbors and go to the big town. When Yehuda was eleven, his father took him by muleback two days' distance to the provincial capital of Gondar, a sprawling, dusty settlement that had preceded Addis Ababa as Ethiopia's capital. For Yehuda, it was his first glimpse of a two-story building, or of an automobile—two were in the town, belonging to an Italian merchant and an English missionary. Most transportation in Gondar, then as now, was by horse-drawn carriage.

Only a few Jewish families lived in the town, in a separate quarter from the predominant Christian community and the smaller Moslem population. Ethiopian Jews who left the village and lived among the gentiles were generally ostracized by their people. They were considered to be contaminated by contact with idolators. In order to reenter a Falasha village, they had to undergo complex ablution rituals to wash away their sins. But some allowance was made for the youths who were forced to go to the town in order to continue their education. And the Gondar connection was an old one—the Jewish quarter there had existed for centuries. In medieval Ethiopia, the Falashas had been forced to live in Gondar, for they were the principal masons and carpenters who built the castles and churches of the emperors. Their descendants still lived there.

Yehuda was excited at first about being in the town of forty thousand people. But he soon encountered directly the prejudice and persecution that the Falashas had suffered intermittently for centuries. Christian children cursed him as *buda* (possessor of the evil eye), killer of Jesus, stranger, descendant of a monstrous Jewish queen of a thousand years ago who burned churches and ravaged the land. The neighbors often wore *juju* bags to ward off the evil eye, and it was believed that the Falashas could turn themselves into hyenas at night, that they devoured Christian women and used their blood for Jewish rituals.

Picturesque Gondar, set between two rivers and surrounded by mauve-colored mountains on three sides, was a nightmarish place for Yehuda. A constant tension of violence prevailed. In the Christian marketplace, criminals were hanged in public every Sabbath and left strung up all day. There were also hangings of opponents of the regime from the huge tree in the center of town, in front of the castle built by Emperor Fasiledes, founder of Gondar. People ate raw meat, always an abomination to the Jews.

The English missionaries in and around Gondar had been trying to convert the Ethiopian Jews to Christianity since the early nineteenth century, and thousands of Falashas over the years had left their religion and people. The relatives Yehuda boarded with told him that the missionaries were successful because "what influences people is money." The missionaries had won converts by providing free education and inexpensive medical attention. Nothing was being done for the Falashas by world Jewish organizations or Israel, Yehuda learned. His relatives, despite living in the town, had remained strictly observant; and Yehuda began to see more clearly that his people's religion was the only safeguard for their preservation.

FOR A BRIEF period in the years immediately following Israel's independence, Polish-born Jacques Faitlovitch, the greatest friend and benefactor of the Ethiopian Jews, had managed to spark some interest in the Falashas among a few rabbis in the Torah Education Division of the Jewish Agency in Jerusalem. An emissary was sent to educate the Falashas about modern Judaism. The rabbi who set up a school in Asmara, Eritrea, later visited the Falasha students in Gondar and was particularly impressed by Yehuda's sharp mind, intense desire for learning, and identification with Israel. Neither the rabbinical authorities nor the Israeli government considered the Falashas to be Jews, and Yehuda told the rabbi that this was a great injustice, that the situation had to be changed.

Soon afterward, just as he reached the age of fourteen, a rare opportunity opened up for Yehuda. Yona Bogala—the gray-haired man of Yehuda's dream—came to Gondar and told him that he was chosen to be among the first group of Falasha youths to be educated in Israel in a program sponsored by a Jewish organization.

At the Kfar Batya youth center in Israel, the young Falashas learned Hebrew and were introduced to rabbinical Judaism in preparation for their return to Ethiopia, where they were expected to pass on their knowledge to their people. Two such groups were sent to Kfar Batya in the 1950s, and most of the total number of twenty-seven youngsters who lived there would one day figure prominently in the story of The Return, as the Ethiopian Jews would call it.

Yehuda wrote lyrical letters home about what he saw in Israel. His only critical remarks were about violations of the Sabbath; he had been shocked to learn that most Israelis were not observant. His grandfather would read the letters to the whole family gathered in the compound around their *tukul*. The women who were kept in isolation in a separate hut during menstruation or after childbirth could also hear. It was an emotional experience and an enchantment for them to learn that Yehuda had visited the reputed tomb of King David on Mount Zion. They recited the Falasha prayer in which David hails "the one who lifted me up from the gates of death so that I may tell His praises in the gates of the daughter of Zion." Yehuda wrote that he was meditating day and night in the law of the Lord. He also had an Israeli girlfriend.

When Yehuda returned to Ethiopia years later, he was in his early twenties and no longer "a Falasha." He had become thoroughly Israeliized, and after a few months in the village, he couldn't endure country life anymore. He went to Addis Ababa and got a job with one of the Israeli companies carrying out major construction, farming, and industrial projects in Ethiopia. Yehuda soon became an indispensable factotum for the Israelis, operating smoothly in the corruption-ridden society. The Israelis were not interested in the Falashas. Only a few of the hundreds of Israelis working in the country had bothered to visit the Falasha villages, and most of them came away feeling that the Beta-Israel were in no way Jewish.

Within a few years, Yehuda had acquired a villa, a car, a wardrobe of silk suits, and a mistress. He liked the fast life but continued to follow his religion's precepts about keeping kosher and honoring the Sabbath. He was generous with his money to both family and friends, and was regarded as a loyal, pious man despite his flashy ways.

One day in 1969, at the height of his career, he decided to abandon it all. He was convinced that his impoverished and persecuted people, whose numbers had dwindled to twenty-five thousand, would soon disappear unless something were done to speed up the long-awaited redemption they prayed for every day. The main threats were from poverty, conversion, and assimilation. But there was also a palpable feeling that many Falashas could face massacre, as had happened in isolated incidents in recent years. Yehuda distributed most of his savings among his family and left for an uncertain future in Israel. He vowed that he would bring them all to the Promised Land if he could acquire Israeli citizenship.

At the time, before the Israeli government's 1975 decision allowing Ethiopian Jews to immigrate to Israel under the Law of Return, it was almost impossible for a Falasha to get even a visa to visit Israel. Yehuda, with his good Israeli and Ethiopian connections, was one of the handful who managed to overcome the obstacles. He was even able to serve in the Israeli army.

At Kfar Batya in the 1950s, he had never experienced prejudice or discrimination. In the army, most of his fellow soldiers were friendly enough, but for the first time in Israel, he also encountered outright hostility, as well as a patronizing attitude by some of the officers and NCOs during basic training. But he was a good soldier and gained their respect, eventually becoming a sergeant. He was stationed in the Sinai.

Yehuda was severely wounded during the War of Attrition—the big gun battles between Egypt and Israel in the years after the 1967 Six-Day War—and was decorated for bravery; but he was still not entitled to the full rights of an Israeli. He was not permitted to

bring his parents to Israel. The only way they could
come to the Holy Land was to masquerade as Christians. Ethiopian pilgrims had no trouble getting
tourist visas from the Israeli embassy in Addis Ababa.
This they did in 1972. But three of Yehuda's brothers, who spurned his advice to wear crosses, were
turned back by the Israeli embassy. Yehuda, who was
still in the service, threatened to call a news conference in Jerusalem and to burn his uniform and dec-
orations unless his brothers were given tourist visas
at the least—an immigrant visa for an Ethiopian Jew
was beyond contemplation. He got what he wanted.

Because of Yehuda's tenacity, he eventually managed to bring dozens of others to Israel. He settled
his brothers and his parents in small housing-project
apartments and managed to get rent subsidies from
the Jewish Agency, the quasi-governmental body in
charge of immigration.

After his army years, Yehuda's concern for the fate
of his people gradually became an obsession, and he
worked full-time to help bring Ethiopian Jews to Israel. The wiry, hard-drinking Yehuda became a guide,
translator, community activist, security-service secret agent, and omnipresent workhorse, one of the
principal connections between "the lost tribe of Dan"
and the rest of Israel.

Yehuda had long wrestled with himself over what
course to follow. He worked for the government but
often found himself among the critics saying that Israel was not doing enough to save the Ethiopian Jews.
His concern was made more urgent by massacres of
Falasha villagers in 1972, 1977, and 1979 by bandits
and local insurgents. At times, Yehuda felt that by
working with the slow-moving Israeli government, he

was further endangering the lives of his people rather than helping them. But at other times, he was convinced that the critics were wrong and that their sometimes reckless words would damage rescue efforts.

In the early 1980s, some of the younger activists among the small community of Ethiopian Jews in Israel accused Yehuda of being a lackey of the government, the Jewish Agency, and the Mossad—the secret service.

But while the "young guard" demonstrated and gave interviews, Yehuda was busy "in the field": in Israel, Ethiopia, Kenya, Paris, Athens, Brussels, New York, and in the Sudan. He haunted the offices of Israeli government leaders who *had* to be made aware of the emergency, and of the consequences if they did not meet it.

He was a Jew from Africa, and a tradition of spiritual unrest flowed in his bloodlines. For a few years in Israel, he had fallen away from the religion. But it came back with a vengeance. As with several other Ethiopian Jews who were working full-time on behalf of their people, his missionary zeal took on messianic overtones. As the number of reports of atrocities against the Beta-Israel increased, he turned more and more to the religion, to Moses and King David and Jeremiah. He quoted a Falasha psalm to a former Mossad official who was now a power in the government: "Therefore, O Lord, remember us who are appointed for death, whom they took captive and prisoners like cattle, and whom they slew like sheep. We cried to God, our Creator, and when we were desolate the Lord listened to our prayers."

Yehuda was constantly on the go, visiting Ethiopian Jews at transit stations and absorption centers around Israel or traveling on some secret mission. Often, he didn't even tell Rina, his Israeli-born wife, where he was going or how many days the trip would last. Sometimes he would wear his army reserves uniform and take a small satchel with him. Rina wouldn't dream of asking him about it. The Ethiopians were the most secretive people she had ever met, and Yehuda was the most secretive of the hundreds she had encountered as a government absorption worker. She never queried him about work connected to the secret service.

Yehuda rarely saw his three children. Every so often, he would take his twelve-year-old son, Ami, and park him at one of the centers while he went about his business. The boy worshipped him and never complained about being ignored or forgotten. Yehuda, in a rare moment, admitted to a friend after a couple of double whiskeys that he simply wasn't a good father. He was essentially a loner, preoccupied and self-centered. Rina knew all that when she married him, knew that it wouldn't be easy, that Yehuda was a man with a mission.

ONE DAY, THIRTY-SIX years after playing the Devil to his sisters, Yehuda felt for a few moments that he was completely out of touch with time. It was a drizzly afternoon in late November 1984 at Ben-Gurion Airport near Tel Aviv. He was disoriented and almost in a trance as he stood before the passengers on the airliner, who were clad in burlap rags or tattered white togas—the traditional Ethiopian garment called *shamma*. They looked as if they had stepped out of the Bible, as he had once looked when he shepherded his flock in the green fields near Ambover. The euphoria over the rescue of his people was tempered by the painful knowledge that many hundreds had died on the way out. But he knew that he had to maintain his composure at such a moment, for a few feet away from him at the entrance of the Boeing 707 stood the prime minister of Israel and his aides, surveying the 250 passengers.

Twenty hours earlier, these Ethiopian Jews were in a sweltering refugee camp between the vast semiarid Sudanese plain and the desert that spreads beneath the supernal Ethiopian mountains. A drought and famine of epic proportions were devastating the land where they had lived for centuries. Millions of lives were threatened, and hundreds of people in the camps were dying every day of malnutrition, dehydration, malaria, typhus, cholera, measles, pneumonia. Then, suddenly, most of the Beta-Israel—the "House of Israel," as the Falashas called themselves—had been plucked from the arms of death.

For a few moments, a strange silence prevailed on the chartered airliner parked at the secret military section of the national airport. Thousands of Ethiopians can sit together without a murmur, for quietness and a shy grace are part of Ethiopia's dominant Amhara culture. But there was more to it than tradition this time. The passengers were stunned, traumatized by their experience. Not one of them had ever seen an airplane before. The last emperor, the man who took the name Haile Selassie ("Power of the Trinity" in Amharic) and who called himself The Lion of Judah and The Chosen of God, brought the first airplanes to Ethiopia in the 1920s, and his people said the craft were instruments of Satan. But there was no doubt in the minds of the Ethiopian Jews that *they* were the Chosen People and that their flight was the work of the God of Israel.

Yehuda, his eyes sparkling, stood before them. Six weeks earlier, just before he learned of the impending airlift, he had been in despair, convinced that nothing substantial would be done to speed up the rescue effort, even though Israeli officials knew that hundreds of Jews were dying in the camps of eastern Sudan. Two months before the airlift, he had spent an hour with an important Foreign Ministry official who expressed his sympathies, relit his pipe, and shrugged his shoulders.

On the hushed airliner, Yehuda raised his arms to welcome the newcomers, as he had been doing every afternoon since the airlift began. "You've arrived in Zion. You are home at last. In Jerusalem!" he told them. He knew they wouldn't recognize the names Ben-Gurion Airport or Tel Aviv, but the word Jerusalem, even more than Zion, was spellbinding.

Most of the passengers assumed that Yehuda, who wore Western clothes and a yarmulke, was simply a black Israeli who happened to know their language. He couldn't be a Falasha like them.

When Yehuda incanted the word Jersualem, it opened up the floodgates of emotion. The Ethiopians applauded wildly, sang songs, laughed, cried. Tears welled in the eyes of Prime Minister Shimon Peres as well, as Yehuda told the tribesmen, "These are the leaders of Israel, the people responsible for bringing you here."

Peres could manage only a few words of greeting as the ailing and infirm were led from the plane. "Shalom, shalom, shalom!" he said, pumping hands.

The people moved down the ramp slowly, most were barefoot and looked starved. One middle-aged man carried his father, a shriveled old man, on his back, as he had done on the long trek from Ethiopia to Sudan, like a black Aeneas. The father, ninety years old, blind and ailing, suddenly came to life, crying out, "We have arrived; we have earned our redemption!" The old man told his son to put him down. He touched the people around him and groped for a handful of ground to kiss but found only tarmac. He viewed the deaths of many hundreds of Ethiopian Jews, including members of his immediate family, as another chapter of the Jewish historical experience—an apocalyptic vision of darkness, sorrow, and ruin that accompanied their salvation.

For the Israelis who were present at the scene—drivers, ground crew, Mossad people, social workers, interpreters, Border Police—the sight of the newcomers raising their hands toward the heavens and prostrating themselves was overwhelming. Most of the Falashas fell to the ground and kissed it, repeating a ritual followed by the waves of new immigrants who had reached the Holy Land from Russia, Yemen, Morocco, Rumania, India.

The Ethiopian immigration was Theodor Herzl's dream punctuated once again, one hundred years after the return to Zion had begun.

THE REDEMPTION FROM Egypt celebrated every Passover and in the daily prayers of the Falashas pointed the way to the future redemption when mankind would be delivered from all oppression, physical and spiritual. Yehuda and his contemporaries had been taught from earliest childhood that only those with a deep, abiding faith, and those whom God had chosen, would return to Zion. During the early 1950s, an occasional Jew from Israel or America would visit the Falasha villages and promote Zionism. Yehuda's grandfather would tell them that it was mere talk, that the time was not ripe.

Yehuda thought about the foresight of his grandfather, now dead, who had said almost forty years earlier that it would be many more long and difficult years—a whole generation—before the Beta-Israel would be redeemed. When Yehuda looked at the new arrivals, who had survived the dangers of jungle, desert, bandits, soldiers, insurgents, and disease, he felt that it was the realization of biblical prophecy. How else could he explain the presence of his eighty-five-year-old aunt, who walked barefoot for three months and then survived eight more months in the worst of the refugee camps, while younger and healthier people did not make it?

As Yehuda led the newcomers from the tarmac to the tables of waiting immigration officials, translators, and social workers, one of the passengers ran up to kiss him on each cheek, doing so over and over again. The frail, emaciated man had brought with him only the clothes on his back, like all of the others. Not a suitcase was to be seen on the airlift flights, just an occasional water bottle or an ancient holy book made of thick, warped parchment. Only later, when the refugees told their stories, would it be learned how precious a water bottle could be. The man was a distant cousin from Yehuda's birthplace, Ambover. Yehuda was overcome with joy.

It was not the first such reunion for Yehuda. In the past nine days, he had encountered—besides his el-

derly aunt and a sister—two of his brothers, two un-
cles, a dozen cousins, and innumerable distant
relatives. All of them had been "released," "delivered" in return for God only knew what. It appeared
that a great deal of money had changed hands at
various levels. The Hebrew word for ransom, for this
kind of redemption, *pedeah*, has the same three-letter
root and the same meaning in ancient Ethiopic. In
Talmudic Judaism, of which the Falashas until recently were unaware, the ransom of hostages is the
holiest of imperatives. But the Ethiopian Jews also
saw their salvation in terms of the biblical *geula*, the
Hebrew word describing Israel's eschatological redemption and thence the redemption of the world.
(The Beta-Israel were not the first to view their immigration in mystic terms. The Yemenite Jews, forty-
three thousand of whom were brought to Israel in the
"Operation Magic Carpet" airlift from Aden in 1950,
still talk in terms of the year of their "redemption"—
events happened so many years before or after "the
redemption.")

It all had been written in the words of the prophets, the Falashas said. Isaiah declared that one day a
present would be brought to the Lord out of Ethiopia—the gift of a people tall and of glossy skin who
would go up to Mount Zion, the exiles ingathered from
Cush. In Zephaniah it was written: "From beyond the
rivers of Ethiopia shall they bring My suppliants, even
the daughter of my dispersed, as Mine offering." (But
the prophet believed that the gentile nations, in whose
midst the Jews were living, would one day surrender
them and bring them back to the land of Israel as an
offering to God and proof of their own conversion to
Judaism.) Yehuda thought of the Midrashic com-

mentary to Psalms, when Israel asked God, "When will you redeem us?" The answer was most fitting in the light of the Falashas' long and anguished history: "When you have sunk to the lowest level, at that time will I redeem you."

2

Strangers

Over the centuries the Beta-Israel made their homes in the northwestern Ethiopian highlands and in the towering mountains, where the heights offered sanctuary in terrain easy to defend. That much is known. But who they are and where they came from is mostly guesswork. The scholars appear to have only a few more clues than the rabbis.

There are at least a dozen theories on the origins of the Falashas, on how and when they acquired their

Judaic beliefs. Orientalist Wolf Leslau, whose *Falasha Anthology* is the seminal work in English on the Ethiopian Jews, believes that the Falashas are descendants of converts whose Jewish teachers came by way of Arabia in the early sixth century, when Judaism was sweeping the region. But much of what is offered as evidence lacks a historical basis and is of a legendary character, coming from reports by Jewish travelers such as Eldad Hadani in the ninth century and Benjamin of Tudela in the twelfth century.

Leading rabbis over the last five centuries have identified the Ethiopian Jews as the Lost Tribe of Dan, one of the Ten Tribes carried away by the Assyrians in 722 B.C.E. (Before the Common Era). But most of the secular scholars agree with the theory put forward by Leslau and the nineteenth-century French Semiticist Joseph Halévy, who said that the Beta-Israel are probably descendants of converts. In part because of linguistic evidence, scholars believe they are related to the Agau tribes, who were perhaps Ethiopia's indigenous people. The Falashas themselves have an oral tradition that says they came "from the west"—by way of Sudan (Cush in ancient times). The prophecy Yehuda once heard from his grandfather that one day the Falashas would return to the Holy Land via the same route by which they came to Ethiopia appears to be an old as well as widespread belief among the Ethiopian Jews.

A leading modern scholar of Ethiopian history, Carlo Conti-Rossini, wrote that "Judaic nuclei" probably existed in Ethiopia before the dominant Semitic tribes were converted to Christianity in the fourth century. He said that the Falashas would then be the descendants of those Judaized Ethiopians who had not converted to Christianity. The Falashas, more than any other tribe, held fast to Judaic beliefs.

Many legends give colorful explanations of the tribe's etiology: the Falashas are the sons of Moses, who reigned as king in Ethiopia after he fled Egypt, or they are the Jews of the Exodus who failed to get across the parted waters of the Red Sea in time and straggled south to Ethiopia along the shore. Some Ethiopian sources say that the Beta-Israel are the progeny of King Solomon and the Queen of Sheba's handmaiden—the Semitic Ethiopian tribes (the Amhara and Tigreans) claim descent from Solomon and the queen. Or they are exiles from the Assyrian conquest, or the progeny of those who left the land of Israel after the Babylonians destroyed the First Temple in 586 B.C.E. One theory is that the Falashas are descendants of Jewish soldiers who were stationed on the Nile island of Elephantine twenty-five hundred years ago—a thousand miles from Falasha country. Another connects them to the sixth-century Jewish kingdom in nearby Yemen ruled by Dhu-Nuwas, son of a Jewish slave. Ethiopia and Arabia, just across the Gate of Tears at the end of the Red Sea, were closely linked for thousands of years, with a great deal of opportunity for intermixing.

According to Josephus, the first-century Jewish historian, Moses once ruled in Ethiopia, which he entered as head of an Egyptian army. He married the daughter of the Ethiopian king after first conquering Saba—Sheba, or Yemen. The tradition that Moses ruled in Ethiopia is also shared by the Ethiopians. The Falashas have a particular reverence for Moses, and at every funeral they recite a moving story about his

death. There would be something highly appropriate
about calling their return to Israel Operation Moses.

The most celebrated meeting between Jew and
Ethiopian is recorded in a few brief lines in the Bible—the story of King Solomon and the Queen of
Sheba, the queen who may have ruled over Ethiopia
and Yemen. The story is undoubtedly grounded in
historical fact. According to the biblical account, the
queen decided to journey to Jerusalem after hearing
about the God of the Jews and the magnificent court
of King Solomon. Her great retinue included camels
laden with precious stones, gold, and spices. She was
awed by Solomon's court and blessed the God of Israel. She gave Solomon 4½ tons of gold for the Temple. Solomon gave her "all her desire"—he made her
pregnant—whereupon she returned to Sheba.

Kabbalists of the Middle Ages would say that the
Queen of Sheba had deceived Solomon and didn't
really accept the God of Israel. She was seen as a great
source of torment for the Jewish people, and she was
regarded as a demon, a succubus. According to the
Kabbala, she is destined to lay waste Rome at the End
of Days, while the Messiah will rebuild Jerusalem
with an amulet made from the gold of Sheba. Christians of the Middle Ages had the opposite image of
the Queen of Sheba—she was portrayed as the Bride
of Christ, the church itself.

Her story is the national epic of Ethiopia, set down
in the fourteenth-century *Kebra Nagast* (Glory of the
Kings), which portrays Sheba as an innocent virgin
seduced and impregnated by the wily, somewhat evil
king of Jerusalem. The object of this book was to prove
that the Ethiopians had replaced the Jews as the
Chosen People.

Their son, Menelik, was said to have stolen the Ark of the Covenant, containing the tablets with the Ten Commandments, from the Temple in Jerusalem and to have brought it to Axum, the Queen of Sheba's "new Zion," the "second Jerusalem" in northern Ethiopia—near Falasha country. In Jewish tradition, the Ark was lost to history after the Babylonian conquest. But the Ethiopians insist it is hidden in their country.

R. E. Cheesman, the explorer of the "jewel of Ethiopia," Lake Tana, said that the Ark was the pivot round which the Ethiopian Church revolved. A replica of the Ark, called *tabot*, is ensconced in every Ethiopian church. The legend of the Ark is the cornerstone of the Ethiopian Christian belief that the Jews, who had rejected "the messiah" and therefore lost possession of the Ark, had been replaced by the Ethiopians as the Elect of God.

THE MYSTERIOUS NINTH-CENTURY traveler Eldad Hadani ("the Danite" in Hebrew) reported that his people, the Lost Tribe of Dan, and three other tribes of Israel had survived in a mountainous area of northeast Africa. They were constantly at war with their neighbors, he wrote in his diaries, "and they slew [the men of Ethiopia], and unto this very day, they fight [with the children of the kingdoms of Ethiopia]." He said that the Israelite tribes had come to "the land of gold" after spending some time in Egypt and that his people lived near an impassable river, where the waters rushed through gorges and mile-deep ravines. Some scholars have conjectured that the legendary Sambatyon River mentioned by the rabbis is the Tekeze, the ancient boundary of the Ethiopian Jews, where Moses was said to have destroyed an Ethiopian dam built to choke off the Nile's headwaters. Eldad Hadani explained that the Israelites who had wandered into exile beyond the Sambatyon "know not the rabbis, for these were of the Second Temple and they did not reach them." He said that they did not read the book of Esther or celebrate Purim (marking Jewish survival under a Persian despot) since they were not included "in the miraculous salvation mentioned in it."

Scholars who are skeptical of Eldad's accounts say that they are only embellishments based on the lives of Jewish rulers such as Dhu-Nuwas of Yemen or on the history of the Khazar people of Eastern Europe.

In the tenth century, a Jewish queen of legendary beauty, Yehudit, or Judith, was said to have conquered northern Ethiopia, including the ancient capital of Axum in Tigre Province. The legend relates that Yehudit destroyed many cathedrals and churches, declaring that she and her husband, who had come from Syria, were Jews. She is said to have dealt a devastating blow to Christianity in Africa and changed the course of Ethiopian history. Her name remains a curse word among Christian Ethiopians today.

There is no historical proof that Queen Yehudit existed or that she was a Falasha, any more than there is proof that her near contemporary, King Arthur of England, presided over the Round Table. Yehudit's descendants were said to have ruled Ethiopia until they were overthrown by the Zagwe dynasty. After the thirteenth century, when the Solomonic dynasty displaced the Zagwes, all Ethiopian rulers claimed descent from King Solomon.

ONLY IN RECENT years, through the study of the Ethiopian Royal Chronicles, has the important influence of the Falashas on general Ethiopian and African history been recognized. As the history of the Beta-Israel begins to emerge from behind the myths and legends, it is possible to trace its outlines and distinguish its most important events. The focus shifts from the question of how Judaism or Jews reached Ethiopia to the question of how the Ethiopian Jews survived despite their isolation for hundreds of years. In terms of the rest of the world, and in the words of Gibbon, Ethiopia "slept for a thousand years." During this long sleep, the Beta-Israel thought that they were the only Jews left in the world.

The earliest reliable references to the Jews of Ethiopia in any Ethiopian source appears to be in the chronicle of King Amda Seyon (the name means "Pillar of Zion"), who reigned from 1313 to 1344. It was written that people who "denied Christ like the Jews who crucified him" offered stiff resistance to the king's expansionist policies, and although temporarily subdued, they rose in revolt around the year 1332. The fact that the first local reference to the Jews of Ethiopia appears in a military context is significant: during a period of over three hundred years, from 1314 to 1632, the primary threat to the survival of the Beta-Israel was military-political as the Christian kings defeated previously independent or semi-independent groups.

Religious differences played only a relatively minor role in provoking the clashes. Political and economic considerations were generally paramount in the wars against Moslems, Jews, animists, and fellow Christians. Consequently, the Ethiopian kings made only sporadic attempts during this period to convert the defeated Jews. Nevertheless, a long-standing "grudge" existed against the Jews. After all, the Ethiopian Christians believed that *they* were the new Chosen People.

The fifteenth-century monarch Yeshaq was the first of the Solomonic kings personally to lead his troops against the Beta-Israel. He appears to have been greatly helped by a split that had developed among the Beta-Israel—between those who advocated a policy of accommodation toward the Christian kings and those who favored continued rebellion. Aided by some of the dissident Beta-Israel leaders, he inflicted a devastating defeat upon rebels from the Semien Mountain region and Dambya. For the first time the defeated Beta-Israel lost their right to own land and were pressured to convert. Yeshaq is said to have issued a decree that "he who is baptized in the Christian religion may inherit the land of his father, otherwise let him be a Falasi." The ethnic name "Falasha"—a stranger, wanderer, or exile—may have originated in this decree. In any case, Yeshaq's reign marked the beginning of a gradual process of Beta-Israel disenfranchisement.

Yeshaq's war against the Jews reached the ears of Jewish travelers to Jerusalem, such as Elijah of Ferrara, an Italian Jew. In 1438 Elijah wrote of his meeting in the holy city with a Falasha who had related to him the story of the long war in the mountains of Ethiopia. In 1489, Obadiah of Bertinoro mentioned Falashas in his letters from Jerusalem. He recorded seeing some Ethiopian Jews in Egypt and revived the story that the Lost Tribes were at war with the legendary Christian monarch of Ethiopia, Prester

John. He reported that the mythical Sambatyon River was located fifty days' journey from Yemen and that it separated the territory of the Children of Moses from the other tribes of Ethiopia.

In the Kabbalistic center of Safad, in northern Israel, as well as in Jerusalem, the wars against the Ethiopian Jews were discussed by Jewish mystics. In 1528 Rabbi Abraham Ben-Eliezer Halevi referred to princes named Gad and Dan in his *Letter on the Secret of the Redemption*. More details about the Lost Tribes and the redemption were given in other letters that the Kabbala sage and his circle sent from Jerusalem to Jews in Italy. This "apocalyptic propaganda," as the eminent scholar Gershom Scholem called it, was inspired by the eschatological mood of the period. Rabbi Halevi wrote that the Falashas were nomadic herdsmen and that they were ruled by two strong kings. He said that the Christian rulers had slain 100,000 Jews but had not succeeded in conquering them.

For centuries, the Beta-Israel were ruled by monarchs who had carved out an independent kingdom in the mountain fastnesses bordered in part by the churning waters of the Tekeze River. According to the Falashas' oral tradition, all of the Falasha kings took the name of Gideon, and Jewish queens all took the name Yehudit. In the Bible, Gideon was a warrior-judge "raised up" by the Lord as a "deliverer for the people of Israel." In a postbiblical apocryphal work, Yehudit was a pious woman who saved the Jews by slaying an enemy general.

After the monarchy came to an end, and in response to their deteriorating political and economic situation, the Beta-Israel devised a number of strat-

egies to ensure their survival. Perhaps most interest-
ing, they adopted and adapted elements from the
surrounding Christian culture in order to develop and
strengthen their specifically Jewish religious identity. A prime example was the appearance in the fifteenth century of Beta-Israel monasticism.

Until recently, Beta-Israel monasticism seemed to
be just one more puzzling aspect of the group's history. There is no doubt that the Falashas acquired
many un-Jewish customs over the centuries and were
heavily influenced by the beliefs of their neighbors—
both Christian and, to a lesser extent, Moslem—just
as there is a heavy Jewish mark on Ethiopian Christianity. But research by scholars such as the American James Quirin have shown that the Beta-Israel
developed monasticism as a means of revitalizing the
moral and ideological basis of their society after their
defeat by Yeshaq. Just at the time when the tribe was
under the greatest pressure, the decision was made
to introduce monasticism, giving select members of
the community the opportunity to devote themselves
to the preservation and articulation of their unique
religious system.

Under the leadership of such converts to Judaism
as Abba Sabra, the Beta-Israel monks began to create a leadership which was an alternative to the increasingly threatened political elite that was formed
around the Beta-Israel monarchy. This newly emerged
religious elite manipulated the Jewish-Christian elements of Ethiopian culture in order to bolster the
Beta-Israel's religious identity and reassert their autonomy.

Late in the fifteenth century, the renowned rabbi
of the Jews in Egypt, David ibn abu Zimra, known as

the "Radbaz," passed judgment in Cairo on the validity of a marriage between an Egyptian Jewish man and a Falasha woman. The Radbaz said that the Falashas were basically Jews, from the tribe of Dan, who had adopted some strange customs. His historic ruling would be the basis five hundred years later for the chief Sephardic rabbi of Israel's recognition of the Beta-Israel as Jews.

THE FALASHAS WERE Ethiopian in every respect other than their religion, the faith that preserved their communal life through the centuries. Like all observant Jews, the Beta-Israel followed laws of diet and cleanliness set out in the Five Books of Moses, but they remained ignorant of the rules of *kashrut* laid down in the rabbinical tradition that was recorded in the Talmud after the Roman destruction of Israel, such as the ban on eating meat and milk products together. The Beta-Israel, following a lunar calendar on the Jewish model, celebrated several festivals similar to those of other Jews, including Passover, Rosh Hashana and Yom Kippur. That they did not know of "later" Jewish holidays, such as Hanukkah and Purim, is seen as evidence that they were cut off from mainstream Judaism before the destruction of the Second Temple in 70 c.e. (Common Era).

In all of their prayers, the Falashas turned in the direction of Jerusalem. The main themes of their worship were often the same as the prayers of other Jews: return to Jerusalem, reestablishment of the duties of the priests once the Temple was rebuilt in messianic times, and constant praise of God and supplication to "deliver me and put me with Thy people, Israel." The focus of their belief has always

been on the God of Israel. The Sabbath, personified
and worshipped as a queen, is called Beloved, Lu-
minous, Vivifying.

Passover, the story of the Exodus from slavery to
freedom, has always been the most meaningful festival for the Falashas, who call it Fasika. Throughout
the prayer cycle, the story of the Exodus is recited
regularly and in great detail—how Moses was ad-
monished by God to lead the Israelites out of Egypt,
the parting of the Red Sea waters and the drowning
of Pharaoh's army, the forty years in the wilderness.
For Jews everywhere, the idea of national freedom
from subjection to other states was the main element in their yearnings for redemption—the essence
of Zionism. The stories and prayers recited during the
Fasika festival conclude with praise to God "who
brought us to this day and did not forget us."

The Beta-Israel have many fasts and festivals of
their own, such as the Seged (the word means "to
bow" in Ge'ez), marking the renewal of the covenant
between God and the Jews after the Babylonian exile. They have an unusually strong belief in the angels, and a lengthy prayer about angels is included
in the daily services. The Fast of Av, commemorating
the destruction of the First Temple by the Babylonians in 586 B.C.E., lasts for seventeen days, during
which the Falashas do not eat from sunrise to sunset
and abstain from meat and milk products. Mainstream observant Jews fast for one day on the ninth
of the Jewish month of Av to commemorate the destruction of both the First and the Second Temple. It
has been said that the reason the Beta-Israel fast was
so much longer was because of their intense mourn-
ing for their own state of exile. The prayers, recited

all day long, lament the destruction of Jerusalem and the exile of the Jews.

Over the centuries, the Beta-Israel produced several works of considerable literary merit, such as *The Commandments of the Sabbath* and *The Book of Angels*. The Ethiopian Jewish scribes also adapted local literary works, excising the obviously Christian passages.

The Falasha priest—*kes*, or *cohen*—was allowed to marry but not to divorce. The priests, who performed circumcisions and marriage and burial ceremonies, conducted services in mud-wattle synagogues built so that the worshipper faced Jerusalem. The priesthood was usually inherited.

Music has always played a prominent role in the Falasha liturgy, and songs of redemption accent the highly emotional content of the Beta-Israel rituals. Gongs, cymbals, drums, and one-string violins accompany prayers of thanksgiving both for the Exodus and for the coming redemption: "Blessed be the Lord, God of Israel, Who performed great miracles, Who delivered us."

Judaism and Christianity parted ways, in Ethiopia and elsewhere, over the question of redemption. In Judaism there was no meaning to redemption of the soul if it was unaccompanied by redemption of the Jews from historical exile. Christians believed that redemption of the soul was the essential accomplishment of their Messiah. Falasha holy men, although completely cut off from the great rabbis who were also in exile, held the view that Jewish life was concerned only with the nonmessianic aspect of redemption, the messianic aspect being entirely up to God.

The Judaism of the Falashas as it developed in an

Ethiopian Christian environment provides a crucial
field of study for understanding the relationship between the two religions, and the question of redemption is a clear expression of the differences. For the
Jews, redemption takes place at the end of time and
on the historical stage. It is a communal, public event.
Christianity perceives redemption in the private,
spiritual world, a "rebirth" within the soul.

The Falashas share with Ethiopian Christians the
Jewish literature that arose between the period of the
Bible and the Talmud, in the first and second centu-
ries of the Common Era. The most important of the
apocrypha and pseudepigrapha for the Ethiopian Jews
are the Book of Enoch and above all—except for the
Old Testament itself—the Book of Jubilees, which
purports to be the secret revelation of God's angel to
Moses on Mount Sinai. The book was originally in
Hebrew, but the only extant complete copies are in
Ge'ez and Latin, both translations from the Greek.
This rather eccentric holy book, which starts and ends
with Moses, has been forgotten everywhere but in
Ethiopia. In it, Moses receives all the disclosures of
history, including the time when God will honor his
promise to redeem his people and dwell among them.

The Commandments of the Sabbath and the story of
the creation of the world are taken from the Book of
Jubilees. Jubilees, "the little Genesis" that was also
a basic text of the Essenes (the sect to which the Dead
Sea Scrolls are attributed), opposes all intimacy with
non-Jews, a key stricture among the Beta-Israel.

According to some traditions, it was in the early
fifteenth century that the Beta-Israel developed their
rules of purity known as *attenkuan*, which means "do
not touch me." This dictated that any member of the

community who had been in contact with outsiders had to purify himself through a series of ritual ablutions before rejoining the community, which gave rise to the Amhara belief that the Falashas "smell of water." In this way, the "contagion" of outside influences could be easily isolated and controlled. A symbolic ritual barrier was thus erected between the Beta-Israel and the outside world.

IF MONASTICISM MADE a major contribution to the Beta-Israel's spiritual survival and *attenkuan* to their communal survival, their increasing concentration in specialized crafts helped ensure their economic survival. The Falashas lost their land gradually over a two-hundred-year period following Yeshaq's decree in the fifteenth century. While most of them remained farmers and worked as tenants for Christian lords, crafts played an increasingly important role in their economic life.

Some of the professions, such as weaving and masonry, carried no social stigma, but the Beta-Israel paid a heavy price for their skill as metalsmiths. In Ethiopia, smiths were associated with demonic spirits. Although their skill was desired because of their ability to repair farm implements and weapons, smiths were thought to have supernatural powers and were called *buda*, possessors of the evil eye. They were pilloried for "fashioning the nails used to crucify Jesus." Many European travelers to Ethiopia over the centuries have written of the killing of Falashas who were thought to be *buda*, and the libel remains strong to this day. Several eyewitnesses have testified that a young Ethiopian Jew, who thought he would be among those saved by Operation Moses, was drawn and quartered in the summer of 1984 by other Ethiopian refugees within sight of the Sudan border. They thought he was *buda*.

The two hundred years after Yeshaq's reign marked a period of adaptation during which the Beta-Israel sought to retain a degree of political autonomy. During the reigns of Zar'a Yaqob (1434–68) and Ba'eda Mariam (1468–78), the Beta-Israel sided with rebel governors against the kings. When Moslem Somalis invaded Ethiopia, the Beta-Israel switched sides several times in the hope of bettering their situation. The political center of the Ethiopian empire moved northward during this period, closer to the Dambya-Gondar region, where most of the Falashas were concentrated. The kings built castles, using Beta-Israel craftsmen, and made increasing demands on the local people. Revolt and rebellion became inevitable. Both Sarsa Dengel (1563–97) and Susenyos (1607–32), fought major wars against the Beta-Israel that are richly documented.

A series of major battles took place somewhere in the Semien Mountains near the Mareb River, where the Falasha rebel leader Redai was defeated by Sarsa Dengel, who brought up cannon supplied by the Portuguese. The Falashas say that when the mountain stronghold was in imminent danger of falling, the defenders, like those at Masada during the Jewish revolt against Rome, committed suicide rather than surrender, throwing themselves into the chasms below.

The Falashas say that their Hebrew holy books were all burned as a result of their final defeat and that this is the reason their liturgy is all in Ge'ez, Ethiopia's Latin. Only a few of the *cohenim*, the Falasha

priests, still understand Ge'ez. It is possible that some
of the lost Hebrew works will be found one day in
the remote monasteries of Tigre or neighboring
provinces, some scholars believe.

Sarsa Dengel was a renowned trader in slaves, and
the Falashas were much in demand. Those he didn't
sell he resettled, including two hundred of the Jews
who were sent to Amba-Warq, "gold mountain"—for
the Jews were always associated with gold in the
minds of the superstitious everywhere. The Ethiopians believed that the Beta-Israel hoarded great
quantities of gold, and they were furious when they
found no treasure at the site of Redai's defeat.

Ethiopia's Christian kings, having acquired fire-
arms from the Portuguese, possessed a clear technological advantage over their foes, and they exploited
it with a vengeance. In 1616 King Susenyos ordered
the extermination of all Jews from Lake Tana to the
Semien Mountains. But in the end, he killed fewer
Jews than did Sarsa Dengel. He defeated the Beta-
Israel resoundingly in several battles, ending the last
vestiges of their independence. Most were sold into
slavery or were forced to convert. Their remaining
lands were confiscated—ownership of land is a vital
symbolic as well as economic right among the dominant Amhara. The defeat was total.

Susenyos's son, Fasilides (1632–67) built his capital of Gondar in the midst of the completely subdued
Beta-Israel, who never again posed a threat. The
number of Falashas dwindled from perhaps 300,000
or 500,000 during their prime to about 200,000 in the
eighteenth century, and to below 30,000 in recent
years.

If the survival of Ethiopian Jewry had depended

upon military prowess and political autonomy, the community probably would not have outlasted its defeat by Susenyos. Religious, communal, and economic developments gave the Beta-Israel alternative means to preserve their identity. During the Gondarine period, from 1632 to 1768, many Falashas lived in relative tranquillity and prosperity. Beta-Israel masons and carpenters built Gondar's castles and churches while other Jews served in the royal army. Beta-Israel women became paint makers, decorators, and ceramicists. In return for their services, the Gondarine kings gave some of the Falashas titles and grants of land. The majority of the tribe continued to live apart from non-Jews in order to maintain their laws of ritual purity. In Gondar itself, separate quarters were established for the Moslems and the Jews.

From 1769 to 1855, Ethiopia was in turbulence; power no longer rested with the emperor in Gondar but with local chiefs and warlords who vied with each other. The Beta-Israel lost almost all the social and economic advantages they had gained during the Gondarine era. In the absence of a strong central government, local leaders were able to seize or purchase their land. Even in those cases where the Beta-Israel continued to hold and work the land, the insecurity of the times made farming extremely difficult. Falasha masons and carpenters were no longer in demand, further eroding the tribe's standing. They were also under increasingly strong pressure to convert.

In 1770 James Bruce, the Scottish explorer of the Blue Nile, "rediscovered" the Jews in the Gondar area north of Lake Tana. In his memoirs Bruce asserted that the Falashas had fought for independence long after the downfall of the last Jewish monarch. He lamented the debased state of the Falashas he met and the sale into slavery of the Falashas' children.

Bruce's books later inspired a group of British missionaries—including several prominent apostate Jews—to set up shop in Falasha country and woo souls to "The Cross of the Redeemer." The most fervent of these missionaries, Henry Stern, discoursed on "the wonderful theme of redemption, which we showed, by numerous quotations, ran like a golden thread through every page of the inspired volume [the Christian Bible]." Stern, driven by messianist beliefs, made definite headway. But by 1863 he had converted only sixty-six Falashas, who were duly baptized into the Ethiopian church, in accordance with an agreement between the emperor and the missionaries. This practice was still being followed in the 1970s, until the Marxist revolution brought about the expulsion of the missionaries.

The nineteenth-century English Protestant missionaries won many souls with their spurious promises that the Amhara would finally accept the Jews if they converted, and by offering invaluable health care and education. Although probably no more than two thousand Falashas converted during the first fifty years of activity by the London Society for Promoting Christianity Amongst the Jews, the missionaries produced a dramatic split in Beta-Israel society.

The missionaries' efforts set off an evangelical reaction among the Beta-Israel religious leaders. In the 1840s Abba Wedaje, the chief monk of Qwara, led a revival to bring his people back to their religion. Twenty years later, a false prophet, a monk from Dambya named Abba Mahari, persuaded thousands of his people to leave Ethiopia *en masse* for the Promised Land. He vowed that the miracles of the Exodus would recur for them. They crossed the Tekeze River and circled the Christian holy city of Axum in Tigre, whose cathedral was said to hold the Ark of the Covenant taken by Menelik from Solomon's Temple. The Falashas believed the Christians would return the Ark to the Jews, who would carry it back to the land of Israel. "To their dismay," a missionary wrote of the 1862 march toward Zion, "they received nothing but blows and insults. Many died of hunger and malaria."

Several of the missionaries, including Stern, were later held captive by the Ethiopian ruler Theodore, a man who had a messianic complex of his own and who soon brought about a war with the English. The publicity surrounding the British expedition in 1868 and the missionaries' activities eventually brought about the initial awakening of the world Jewish community to "the lost tribe" of black African Jews.

In 1864 the revered Rabbi Azriel Hildesheimer of Germany, founder of the Agudat Israel sect of Orthodox Jews, urged that a special mission be undertaken to assist the Falashas. Three years later the famed Semiticist Joseph Halévy was sent by a French-Jewish organization to report on the missionaries' attempts to evangelize Jews in northwestern Ethiopia. He was greatly moved upon meeting the Beta-Israel and told them, "I am like you, an Israelite . . . a white Falasha." This is exactly what Stern, the apostate Jew, had said to them, and they were reluctant to talk to Halévy. But the Falashas, overcoming their distrust, sent two youths back with him to be educated in Europe.

Halévy's example inspired one of his students at the

Sorbonne, Jacques Faitlovitch, to continue helping the Ethiopian Jews. In 1904 Faitlovitch, with aid from Baron Edmond de Rothschild and Chief Rabbi Zadoc Kahn of Paris, began teaching Falashas in the villages around Gondar and later took several youths to Europe and Palestine to be educated. Upon his return to France, Faitlovitch submitted a report to Rothschild saying that "the Falashas are really Jews. They have the same aspirations that we do; they believe, like us, that they are the future of Israel. . . . They are an active, intelligent, moral people, with a thirst for learning." He implored the philanthropist to help the black Jews, but this never came about. In 1906 Faitlovitch got the signatures of forty-four leading European rabbis on a letter proclaiming the Falashas "our flesh and blood" and expressing the hope that they would be brought to Zion. But two years later, the French Jewish community sent Rabbi Haim Nahoum to Ethiopia to report on the Falashas. He stated categorically that they were not Jews, that they were happy where they were, and that there was no need to teach them modern Judaism.

In reaction to Rabbi Nahoum's report, Faitlovitch called the Falashas "those martyrs of Judaism" and persisted in his efforts to bring them into the Jewish mainstream. In the 1920s, Faitlovitch and his sister Leah ran a school in Abbis Ababa for Ethiopian Jews, which operated until it was ordered closed down during the Italian occupation. Faitlovitch worked unceasingly to persuade world Jewry to come to the assistance of their brethren in Ethiopia. At the same time, he sought to close the gap between the Beta-Israel and other Jews by raising their educational standards and reforming their religious practice.

Faitlovitch devoted his entire life to the Ethiopian

Jews, and when he died in 1955 he left his large house in Tel Aviv to the Beta-Israel community. Among Faitlovitch's students were Professor Tamrat Emmanuel, who eventually became a diplomat and adviser to Haile Selassie, and Tadessa Yacob, who became Ethiopia's finance minister.

Another student, linguist and educator Yona Bogala, became a leader of his people and the key liaison with world Jewry.

3

The Teacher

Although the Beta-Israel had no official leader, Yona Bogala became the chief spokesman for his people in the 1950s. Yona emerged as a leader because of his position as a high government education official, his reputation as a scholar—including knowledge of Hebrew, Yiddish, French, German, Italian, English, and several Ethiopian languages—and an impressive, diplomatic bearing.

In the years before 1979, when he immigrated to

41

Israel at age seventy-one, Yona steered a cautious course through sometimes treacherous social and political waters. At times, he was sharply criticized by various tribal factions and by outsiders. In retrospect, it was almost inevitable that world Jewry's desire for a single representative of the Falashas would clash with the community's decentralized structure. To this day, many Tigreans accuse the Gondarine Yona of having ignored their needs. Some priests believe he attempted to undermine their authority. These criticisms notwithstanding, the major result of Yona's efforts was to help preserve and prepare his people for what he would call the "miraculous events" of Operation Moses. Yeshayahu Ben-Baruch, one of the younger generation of Ethiopian Jewish leaders in Israel, would say of Yona: "Without him, the rescue would not have happened."

Yona Bogala was born in 1908 in Wallaca village, just outside Gondar. His father was a weaver, and during the rainy season, he ploughed a small patch of land belonging to a Christian nobleman attached to the emperor's court. The family, including eleven children, lived in a traditional Ethiopian *tukul*, and scratched out their existence growing *teff*. Like almost all of the Beta-Israel, they were virtual serfs who paid most of their crops to the feudal landowner.

In 1921 Jacques Faitlovitch spent several months in Wallaca, and Yona studied Hebrew with him every day after sunset. When Faitlovitch proposed to take Yona, along with some of his other students, to Palestine and Europe to be educated, Yona's parents agreed reluctantly. Yona and the three other youths who were selected were part of the "student chain" that had begun in the 1860s. It would prove to be a vital step toward the eventual emigration of the Beta-Israel. For after several years abroad, most of these students returned to Ethiopia, where a few taught Hebrew and spread the Zionist message.

Yona studied for over two years at a Jerusalem yeshiva and then went with Faitlovitch to Frankfurt, where he studied German and learned Yiddish. In his midteens, he continued his education at a Jewish school in Switzerland, studying French and Hebrew.

Faitlovitch's very first pupil, Tamrat Emmanuel, had become a professor and director of the teacher-training school set up by Faitlovitch and his sister in Addis Ababa in 1924; and Yona, after completing his education, joined Tamrat as his assistant and head teacher. The school was set up in a compound with a house and several *tukuls*, which served as class-rooms and dormitories. The first students were chil-dren of Falasha families who had been forcibly brought to Addis in the 1890s by Emperor Menelik II to help build palaces and churches. The opening of a Jewish school in the capital a generation later was regarded by these families as a minor wonder that would preserve their children's Jewish identity. Word of the school also reached the Gondar area, and sev-eral youths walked hundreds of miles south to study at Faitlovitch's institution, which eventually housed eighty Beta-Israel students from all around the country.

After two years of study, graduates were sent out to start schools in the main Falasha villages. From 1924 to 1935, about forty of the more gifted students were taken to Palestine, France, Germany, England, and other countries. The opening of Jewish schools in the capital and in the Falasha villages created a

strong negative reaction among the Ethiopian clergy
and local officials. The clergy and Protestant missionaries petitioned Emperor Haile Selassie and provincial governors to close the schools; in several cases,
teachers in the provinces were imprisoned and their
students dispersed. In 1936, when the Italians occu-
pied Ethiopia, Tamrat, who was on the Fascists'
wanted list, fled to England; and Yona, in addition
to teaching, took over administering the college, until the Italians shut it down. Five of the school's
teachers and outstanding students were imprisoned
by the Italians and later murdered. The Italians also
executed thirty-three Ethiopian Jews in an incident
in the Woggera region, where the Ethiopians had
carried on a guerrilla war against the invaders.

Yona went to work for coffee merchants. He had to
earn enough to take care of sixty Jewish students from
the Gondar area who still lived in Addis Ababa after
the school was closed and who continued to depend
on him. In the privacy of his home he went on tutor-
ing them in Hebrew and other subjects.

Two years later, after the Italians intercepted an
incriminating letter he had sent to Tamrat, Yona became a fugitive. He fled to the south. Yona lived
among the Oromo—who were then called by the de-
rogatory name Galla— learned their language and
worked in the gold mines of Wallaga. There were
legends that these were the same deposits mined in
the days of the Queen of Sheba, that this place was
the "Ophir" mentioned in the Bible. Yona eventually
became chief supervisor of the mines.

When the Italians withdrew from Ethiopia in 1941,
Yona went back to the capital and became head of
the Education Ministry's Department of Schools. But

shortly after Haile Selassie expanded the office to include supervision of schools run by the Christian missionaries, Yona read a report that four thousand Falashas, about one-eighth of the Jewish community, had been baptized in these institutions. He resigned in anger and vowed to devote himself to preserving his people's identity.

In the 1950s, with the aid of funds from the Jewish Agency, he helped set up and run a teacher-training school in Asmara, Eritrea, which was later transferred to the village of Wuzava, near Ambover, the largest Beta-Israel village. The Asmara buildings—a synagogue, dormitories, classrooms, a kitchen and dining room—were erected by Ethiopian Jews from all of the surrounding communities. Jewish Agency funds helped maintain the facilities. But the school soon aroused the suspicion of the Beta-Israel's Christian neighbors, who burned down two of the buildings in 1958. The authorities refused to help the Falashas, who were forced to close the boarding school and send the students home. Around the same time, the Jewish Agency decided to cut off most of its aid to Falasha schools, a move that was welcomed by the English evangelical missionary chief, Eric Payne.

Under Yona's guidance the Beta-Israel, relying on their own meager resources, set up a new central school in Ambover with teachers who had returned from Kfar Batya in Israel. These teachers, like Yehuda, had become thoroughly Westernized during their long stay at Kfar Batya and only reluctantly agreed to live in Ethiopia. But Yona and other Beta-Israel leaders emphasized the teachers' importance to the community, and most of the Kfar Batya veterans came around to his viewpoint. They spent the next twenty-five years teaching Hebrew, introducing the Beta-Israel to the customs of other Jews, and waiting for the time when they could return to Israel.

Ambover, which became the hub of the Falasha villages scattered over several provinces, was founded in 1936 during the Italian occupation. The village, located in a pastoral setting a couple of hours' drive by Land-Rover or two days' walk from Gondar, became Yona Bogala's second "base of operations" after Addis Ababa and was the focal point for the Zionist movement. The mud-wattle huts of the village are clustered around a hill on whose crest stands the grammar school that drew Falasha children from the whole region. The younger generation was clearly inspired by the Zionist zeal of the Kfar Batya veterans, and the introduction of Zionist ideology reinforced the Beta-Israel's religious longings for redemption. But it was a quiet and gradual process in the 1960s, bearing Yona Bogala's mark.

Because of poverty, disease, missionary activity, and sporadic killings, the Falashas were indeed a threatened people, but by the 1970s, there was a small measure of "Zionist hype" as well. A number of young Falashas in Gondar and the main villages, in their contacts with visitors from the outside Jewish world, began to portray their people's plight in Western terms of anti-Semitism. Some engaged in hyperbole. Several Jewish visitors from Israel, England, and America, hearing of the atrocities and the general plight of the Beta-Israel, promised the Falashas that the Jews of the world would help them get to Israel one day.

Atrocities *were* committed against the Jews, and the

tendency to exaggerate was understandable. For behind the blur of fact and fiction, it was clear that the Falashas, their numbers having steadily declined over the centuries, were eventually doomed to die out. Impoverishment added to their concern. Because of their abject poverty, many Falashas had to sell their rifles—worth about two years' wages on the local market—and thus became more vulnerable than ever in a savage, chaotic environment.

Yona Bogala regularly appealed to prominent rabbis around the world to reach a conclusive decision regarding the Falashas' Jewishness. In his correspondence, he quoted to them all of the well-known rulings by rabbis such as the renowned Radbaz. He also cited the 1921 statement by the first chief rabbi of Palestine, Avraham Yitzhak Hacohen Kook, the most important figure in modern Judaism, who urged world Jewry "to save our Falasha brethren from extinction." Kook, who believed that the process of the final redemption had begun, said that it was a holy obligation to bring the Falashas' children to Palestine. But Rabbi Kook's important statement, which had been elicited by Faitlovitch, still fell short of official rabbinical recognition of the Falashas as Jews.

The Jewish aid Yona Bogala dispensed to thousands of Falashas was skimpy indeed—about $30,000 a year, and never exceeding $50,000. Most of it came from the Falasha Welfare Association in England, headed by *Jewish Chronicle* publisher David Kessler. Aid would also come from an American support committee that Faitlovitch had started in the 1920s to "rehabilitate our co-religionists" and that was rejuvenated in April 1974 by an elderly Zionist fundraiser and firebrand, Graenum Berger, who called his

group the American Association for Ethiopian Jews.
That same month, major articles appeared in the
magazines of the *Jerusalem Post* and *Ha'aretz* describing the Falashas' plight in Ethiopia, their strong
desire to immigrate to Israel, and Israeli officials'
negative reactions to the idea. The attitude that then
prevailed in Israel was exemplified by the late Yisrael Yeshayahu, longtime Speaker of the Knesset, who
had visited the Falashas in the 1950s and recom-
mended that Ethiopian Jews convert to Christianity
in order to solve their problems.

The Israeli government did not consider itself responsible for sending aid to the Falashas. Although
one Israeli doctor, Dan Harel, was sent in the early
sixties on a two-year mission to help the Ethiopian
Jews and was a great success, no one replaced him.
Several Israeli medical teams worked in Ethiopia in
those years, even in Gondar itself, but no aid was
designated for the Beta-Israel, who depended on the
English missionaries for medical care. The missionaries, who carried on in the tradition of nineteenth-
century predecessors such as J. M. Flad and Henry
Stern, saved many lives with their medical care. But
the Jews charged that they "bought souls" with
money and various inducements. This undoubtedly
happened, and Roger Cowley, who was the chief
missionary to the Ethiopian Jews in the years 1963–
78, would say some years later that "as a Christian,
I would disapprove of such practices." Cowley, whose
missionaries converted five hundred to one thousand
Falashas during his fifteen-year stay in Ethiopia,
would admit that "it is understandable that Jews re-
gard Christian missionary work as repugnant." He
would also not deny that Falashas who converted were

never really accepted by Christian Ethiopians, who always recalled their Beta-Israel origins.

DURING THE YEARS when the Beta-Israel were not considered Jewish by the Israeli government, the embassy in Addis Ababa consistently turned back Falashas who wished to travel to Israel. Those who were determined to come—like Yehuda's parents—had had to pretend that they were Christian pilgrims in order to get visas. Israel was officially "unenthusiastic" about the black Jews, in the phrase chosen by Foreign Ministry officials and members of the cabinet.

In the 1970s Yona Bogala became increasingly critical of the Israeli government for not moving fast enough to recognize the Falashas as Jews and helping them to immigrate, but his approach was always diplomatic. He believed in the values of negotiation and compromise. His primary goal was to educate, to prepare his people for the day when they would be brought to Israel. But he had learned that the Beta-Israel would have to push for their *aliyah*—"ascension," or immigration, to Israel.

The long effort by Faitlovitch, Yona Bogala, and others to get important rabbis to issue statements about the Falashas finally paid off on February 9, 1973, when Israel's chief Sephardic rabbi, Ovadia Yosef, ruled that the Falashas were Jews according to Halacha, the Jewish law. The rabbi's statement was recorded in a letter to Hezi Ovadia, a controversial former career soldier of Yemenite extraction who had headed an Israeli pro-Falasha committee. The rabbi said that he had come to the conclusion that the "Falashas are descendants of the Tribe of Israel who went southward to Ethiopia" and that great sages such as the Radbaz, Rabbi Hildesheimer, Rabbi Kook, and Kook's successor as chief Ashkenazic rabbi, Yitzhak Halevi Herzog, were correct in saying that the Falashas were of the Tribe of Dan. "I, too, . . . have investigated and inquired well into [these matters] . . . and have decided that in my humble opinion, the Falashas are Jews, whom it is our duty to redeem from assimilation, to hasten their immigration to Israel, to educate them in the spirit of our holy Torah and to make them partners in the building of our sacred land. I am certain that the government institutions and the Jewish Agency, as well as organizations in Israel and the diaspora, will help us to the best of our ability in this holy task . . . the *mitzvah* of redeeming the souls of our people . . . for everyone who saves one soul in Israel, it is as if he had saved the whole world."

It was the key that opened the door to Operation Moses.

Israel's great scholar of the Talmud Rabbi Adin Steinzalz agreed wholeheartedly with Ovadia Yosef's decision but said soon afterward that the Falashas would have significant problems if they ever immigrated: "The fact that Hebrew is not their holy tongue by itself creates a very great difference in perception between them and other Jews," he told me, "and they will have great trouble if they ever come to Israel."

FOR THE FALASHAS, there were more immediate hurdles. Ethiopia was at one time the linchpin of Israel's foreign policy in Africa. Israel built factories and established large farms in Haile Selassie's Ethiopia and engaged in joint enterprises in transportation, education, medicine, and geology. The Mossad and the

Israel Defense Forces advised the Ethiopian army and the Imperial Ethiopian Police as well.

Strong ties were maintained between Israel and Ethiopia even after Haile Selassie broke off formal relations at the time of the 1973 Yom Kippur War. This continued until his downfall the next year, and for several years thereafter. Marxist Ethiopia abstained in the "Zionism is racism" vote in the United Nations, and Israel supplied arms to the revolutionary government. These ties later deteriorated, although there continued to be quiet cooperation in some fields. Up until the 1980s, Israel was reluctant to sacrifice its ties with Ethiopia over the Falashas.

Ethiopia entered its period of great turmoil when it was revealed in 1973 that the feudal regime had suppressed news of a drought and famine that had killed a quarter of a million people in the north. Widespread chaos soon followed. In Falasha country, many Jews were robbed and forced from their farms by several of the absentee landlords in the months immediately preceding the revolution. In general, the landlords of the north owned far smaller tracts of land than the landowners of southern Ethiopia, and the northern aristocrats were more tenacious and bloodthirsty when it came to control over their property.

There were reports that Jewish graveyards were ploughed up and the remains burned or thrown into the rivers. In May of 1973, a Falasha wrote to an official in the World Jewish Congress that "the Christians have started to kill us. They have told us to move from their lands and some of us left the place. The Christians are saying we are sucking their blood. Many of our people were killed a few weeks ago. Please help us as you do the other Jews. If you will not help us quickly, it is evident for everybody we will not be anymore in this world."

Because of the difficult terrain and the lack of communications in the area, it was impossible to verify the reports at the time, although there was no doubt that over thirty Jews were massacred in a village in the Lasta region. Hundreds of Falashas in the Wollo, Semien, and Woggera areas had been evicted from their lands in 1972 and their houses burned. But Israeli officials who were skeptical about the reports said that the Falashas were probably exaggerating their plight because of their desperation to get to Israel. They stated that murder was an everyday occurrence in Ethiopia and that there was no evidence that the Falashas had been singled out for persecution. The general population of northwestern Ethiopia is extremely nationalistic, and all minorities there, not only the Jews, have suffered persecution.

In July 1973, Yona Bogala and other Falasha elders wrote an appeal to the emperor begging him to stop the killings, the destruction of property, and the expulsions from Beta-Israel farms. No action was taken. Still, many Falashas preferred "the devil you know," fearing that whoever succeeded the emperor would be worse.

In reaction to the new wave of persecution in Ethiopia, the small community of Falashas living in Israel—about 150 in the early 1970s—organized themselves and became effectively active for the first time. One of Yona Bogala's sons, Zecharia Yona, joined with Yehuda as a leader of the movement to make Israelis and Jews everywhere aware of the dire situation of the Ethiopian Jews. In a press interview, he asserted that the world Jewish organizations knew all about the reports of pogroms but that they either refused to believe the Falashas or said that it would make matters worse if they took a strong stand. He warned that his people were disappearing, that they were threatened by the landlords, Christian neighbors, poverty, famine, disease, and the missionaries who were converting growing numbers.

The Falashas had no protection against eviction. In a few instances, a Falasha was allowed to bring his case to court, but the judges always found in favor of the church—the biggest landowner next to the emperor—or the other landlords. For in matters of land, despite some exceptions, the Falashas were regarded as "eternally landless" and therefore without any property rights whatsoever.

Because the landlords often took up to four-fifths of the crops from their Falasha sharecroppers, about three out of four Beta-Israel families were forced to supplement their farming income by engaging in craftwork. Their income was far below the national average of about $120 a year, one of the world's lowest. So they were among the poorest of the poor in a place of "hunger, ignorance and disease bestowing their bounty all over the country," in the words of Ethiopian novelist Danachew Worku.

In early 1974 a wave of strikes, protests, and rumblings in the armed forces finally laid low The Lion of Judah, who was deposed in September of that year. The military took over in the form of a mysterious group of 120 men who called themselves the Dergue (committee). Within four years of the revolution, there would be only forty surviving committeemen. On December 20, three months after the emperor was taken away from his palace in a beat-up Volkswa-

gen, the Dergue declared that Ethiopia was a socialist state.

One of the first major acts of the new revolutionary leaders was to declare the nationalization of land,
which was instituted on March 4, 1975, a year of great
hope for the hitherto landless Beta-Israel. In Jerusalem a week later, on March 11, an interministerial
committee of the Israeli government finally ruled that
the Falashas were Jews under the Law of Return, entitled to automatic citizenship and full benefits. A poll
conducted by the Hebrew University showed that
most Israelis favored immigration of the Beta-Israel,
although there was no real movement to bring this
about—it was basically a remote subject to the harried and harassed Israeli public. When the news of
the Jerusalem government's decision reached Ethiopia, hundreds of Falashas sold their meager belongings and came down from the mountain villages to
await a hoped-for "magic carpet" that they imag-
ined would take them to Israel. But no planes came;
and after waiting for a few days, the people went back
to their huts. Some of the religious leaders, after
consulting with Yona Bogala, told their people that
they would have to wait longer for their redemption,
that it was like 1948, a false start.

Within weeks of the Israeli government's decision,
the first clandestine attempt to bring Falashas to Israel was aborted after it was announced to the press
that the Jewish Agency would pay for several flights
of Ethiopian Jews who wished to go to Israel and that
the immigration was already under way. In the wake
of the foul-up, the subject of Ethiopian Jews was put
under the supervision of the military censor, as is the
case with other threatened Jewish communities. The
Beta-Israel's supporters generally welcomed this

move, but some cynical commentators said that the censorship would simply make it easier for Israel to delay taking any substantive action and to suppress critical press reactions.

In early 1977, a former cabinet minister, Shulamit Aloni, charged in the Knesset that there was "a conspiracy of silence" about the Falashas. She claimed that the Labor party government had buckled under to pressure from anti-Falasha members of its coalition partner, the National Religious party, led by Minister Yosef Burg. In March of that year, the government responded by issuing an official statement that reaffirmed the 1975 decision recognizing the Beta-Israel as Jews. A few months later, Menachem Begin and the Likud defeated the Labor party for the first time since the establishment of the state and took over the government. Begin became the first major government leader to meet with representatives of the Falashas in Israel. In private discussions with Yehuda, Zecharia Yona, and other Beta-Israel leaders, Begin declared that "the Falasha community is one of the most ancient in the Jewish dispersion, and we must bring them home."

An arms deal was worked out with the regime of Ethiopian dictator Colonel Mengistu Haile-Mariam, which was then hard-pressed by the secessionist war in Eritrea and war with Somalia in the Ogaden desert. The Ethiopians agreed to allow small groups of Falashas to fly to Israel, on the condition that complete secrecy be maintained. On August 25, 1977, sixty Falashas arrived at the military section of Ben-Gurion Airport. But there would be only one more such flight.

In February 1978, Foreign Minister Moshe Dayan, in a "slip of the tongue" in Geneva, announced to the world that Israel had been arming Ethiopia in its war against Somalia. Mengistu, a great admirer of Israel in most respects, was enraged by Dayan's gaffe and told a visiting American official that one could not trust the Israelis because "'they can't keep a secret." He ordered clandestine flights of Ethiopian Jews halted. The American official, one of the key people later responsible for securing American aid to Israel for the Ethiopian Jews, felt that the Israeli government at that time was "not really anxious to help get the Falashas out. I'm very happy that that attitude changed."

But from 1979 on, the government of Menachem Begin did try hard to reestablish the links broken over the Dayan affair. Contacts were maintained through every possible diplomatic channel. According to one source, Begin asked American industrialist Armand Hammer to solicit help, through his connections with the Soviets and with Mengistu's friend Fidel Castro, in influencing Marxist Ethiopia to ease the plight of its Jews. However, nothing came of this. The "Falasha question" was transferred from the Jewish Agency to the Prime Minister's Office and the Mossad, and the agency had only a peripheral role to play in the following years. Meanwhile, the small but vocal American Association for Ethiopian Jews, impatient with the lack of progress in bringing Falashas to Israel, stepped up its publicity campaign among American Jews to pressure Israel to take action. It also undertook immigration efforts of its own. Yona Bogala, the teacher who had devoted his life to help his people, was among the scores of Ethiopian Jews who reached Israel through the American group's efforts.

ALTHOUGH THE REVOLUTION in Ethiopia gave the Falashas the right to own land for the first time in centuries, it didn't provide them with the opportunity to exercise that right. Much of the Gondar and Tigre regions were under the control of right- and left-wing insurgents. The Dergue also had inherited the problems of the Eritrean and Somali conflicts, as well as the chronic drought and famine.

The "white" reactionary forces of the Ethiopian Democratic Union, led by members of the deposed emperor's family and other landlords, killed scores of Falashas and forced thousands from their homes in the late 1970s. The attacks against the Beta-Israel were particularly vengeful, perhaps because of their servant status in the eyes of the deposed aristocrats. The ragged army of the EDU took over one Beta-Israel settlement and carried away the metalsmiths and potters in chains to be sold in the slave trade that still thrives in the Horn of Africa. (Slavery was made illegal in Ethiopia in 1950 and in neighboring Saudi Arabia in 1962, but it still goes on, according to the UN-affiliated Anti-Slavery League headquartered in London.) The remaining village women were raped and mutilated—hands and breasts cut off—and the men were castrated. Elderly people were tied to thorny bushes and left to die in the sun.

If there were some distorted versions of these atrocity reports in the Western Jewish press, such as claims that a "holocaust" was under way, they stemmed probably from a desire to see the Falashas' wishes to immigrate to Israel fulfilled. Obviously, this was offensive to Ethiopia. As a consequence, the Ethiopian government's general ban on emigration was even more strictly applied to the Falashas.

The Beta-Israel were also singled out for attack by the rebel leftists of the Ethiopian Peoples Revolutionary party, led by Marxist intellectuals, many of whom had studied in Europe and America. Natural disasters also affected the people of northwest Ethiopia, as the drought and famine conditions worsened. The EPRP unleashed a wave of assassinations of scores of Dergue members and their supporters. In response, Colonel Mengistu instituted the officially sanctioned "Red Terror" and systematically liquidated a large percentage of his country's educated citizens—at least five thousand people. High school students—"immature sons of the feudal classes"— were sexually tortured, shot, or thrown out of tall buildings or into vats of boiling oil, according to Amnesty International. When one of his ministers disagreed with him at a cabinet session, Mengistu drew a pistol and shot him dead.

Terror and counterterror spread from the urban centers to the countryside. Signs in Amharic were draped over the bodies: "May the Red Terror Glow Brighter." Many Falashas were reportedly slain in 1977 and 1978.

One Falasha teenager in Addis Ababa who managed to escape "the sword of the Ethiopian Revolution" told me shortly afterward of a former army officer who lived in the house next door to him with his wife and six sons. All six boys were arrested and summarily executed over the May Day weekend of 1977. The retired officer and his wife, like thousands of other parents, got their children's clothes back, blackened and full of bullet holes. If they wanted to claim the body, they had to pay the equivalent of twenty-five dollars for each "mark of death." If the son's body had ten bullet holes, it would cost the father twice the per capita annual income in Ethiopia to get it back.

Addis Ababa and the main towns had become wired with tension and fear. The national radio introduced its frequent execution announcements with a piercing war song. The military regime organized the riffraff "lumpen" of the streets into *kebeles*, thirty thousand cells that became vigilante groups in the urban centers. Every Ethiopian, not just the Falashas, had cause to wish for escape from the brutal reality of his country. The difference was that the Ethiopian Jews had a place to go to—the refuge of Israel.

Both the reactionary EDU and the Jacobin EPRP were finally brought under control by 1980, the year that the new drought became severe. The man who was most responsible for defeating them, Major Malaku Tafara, a member of the ruling Dergue, became governor of Gondar Province. Malaku was said to have had a personal grudge against the Falashas as well.

Over the years, the Ethiopian revolutionary government's attitude to the Beta-Israel had been checkered: it tried to ease some of the Falashas' problems but created others. The national land reform embraced the landless Jews but also set the disenfranchised landlords against the Falashas. Major Malaku restricted the practice of the Beta-Israel's religion, banned the teaching of Hebrew, and closed off Falasha villages to visitors for many months at a time. The Beta-Israel's Christian neighbors began to blame the Jews for the drought and famine that was causing havoc, especially in the Tigre and Wollo provinces, but in Gondar and elsewhere as well. In 1980, one prominent Falasha who worked in Gondar town for the Jewish-run Organization for Rehabilitation Training was murdered by security personnel. An Israeli who headed the ORT program, which was established in 1977 as a training and rural development project for the general population of Gondar Province, reported in 1978 that slave raids were directed against the Falashas of Woggera around Dabat.

ORT, the only Jewish organization that the revolutionary regime permitted to operate in Ethiopia, ran twenty Falasha schools and helped a few hundred Falasha farmers. But some Falasha supporters in the United States and Israel sharply criticized ORT for "contributing to the destruction of the tribe" by working closely with the Ethiopian government. (Allegations of financial wrongdoing also were made. But an unofficial inquiry conducted in Israel found no basis for the allegations.) ORT was expelled from Ethiopia in 1981, and even its harshest critics later conceded that it proved a significant loss to the well-being of the Falashas and other Ethiopians in Gondar Province. Behind the ORT dispute was the belief by sometimes overzealous Zionists that there is only one solution to the "Jewish problem"—*aliyah* to Israel. On the other hand, there were those who believed that the Falashas should be "preserved in their natural environment," that they would become extinct just as quickly if they were brought to Israel. In the often terrifying atmosphere of revolutionary Ethiopia, this debate became academic.

GROWING NUMBERS OF Falashas joined the stream of Ethiopians fleeing westward from the wave of persecution and government repression. Most of those who were caught on the way to Sudan were tortured, and several were permanently crippled by guards who wielded bastinadoes—wooden cudgels—

to beat the soles of the feet until they turned to raw flesh. All of the Falasha teachers who had been educated in the 1950s in Israel were tortured, and some of them spent years in prison.

In Israel members of the Falasha community, encouraged by the American Association for Ethiopian Jews, demonstrated in January 1979 and again in October of that year against the government and the Jewish Agency, saying that not enough was being done to bring the Beta-Israel "home." Yehuda, one of the leaders of the protests, told a press conference that "when the Emperor Haile Selassie was in power, they told us not to make noise and to let them handle things quietly to keep relations between the two countries friendly. They also claimed that the emperor refused to let Jews leave, though when the emperor was asked in specific cases he did give permission. Now, with the military government in power there, they still tell us to keep quiet about it. There has been debate here over the past few weeks about whether hundreds or thousands of Falashas have been killed or sold into slavery. Isn't it enough that Jews are being killed and enslaved? Isn't that enough reason for the Jewish people and the Israeli government to act?"

In response to the charges, a Jewish Agency spokesman said that "a great deal is being done." Prime Minister Begin met again with Yehuda and with Yona Bogala's son and two other Beta-Israel leaders and told them, "First, there is no question about your Jewishness; you are our brothers, our flesh and blood. So the Israeli government has done, is doing and will continue to do its best in searching for ways to bring our brothers here to their home-

land. We are fully aware of their plight, so we will
not let our brothers suffer, but the critical problem
is lack of direct communication with the Ethiopian
leader. Despite this, we work very hard to save the
Falashas."

In November 1979 Yona Bogala and three other
Falasha leaders went to Montreal to address two
thousand representatives of Jewish federations. In an
emotional speech, Yona blamed certain Israeli officials and Jewish organizations for obstructing the
rescue of the Beta-Israel, and said, "Our final hour is
near. Until when shall we cry?"

Israel's secret services managed to bring a few
hundred Falashas to Israel in the next two years, but
the process was agonizingly slow. Demonstrations by
Israeli Falashas were renewed in December 1981,
when there were some fourteen hundred Ethiopian
Jews in Israel.

An American delegation sent to Ethiopia by the
State Department in 1981 reported that the Falashas
were worse off than other minorities in Gondar Province, although the extent of the reported atrocities was
considered to be exaggerated. Around the same period, Gondar governor Malaku, in addition to impos-
ing the restrictions on the Falashas' freedom of
religion and movement, ordered public burnings of
Hebrew books. One Israeli Falasha compared it to the
actions of the Ethiopian ruler Sarsa Dengel in the
sixteenth century.

The revolutionary regime had declared that its aim
was to further the rights of the nationalities and minorities, yet nationalism still held sway, as it had
under the emperor. The regime attempted to destroy
the culture and religion of several minorities. Jews,

Catholics, Jehovah's Witnesses, and others did not have equal religious rights with Moslems and members of the Ethiopian church.

Major Malaku was replaced as governor of Gondar in 1983 by Wesayehu Sahalu, who at first welcomed Western Jewish visitors. Soon after his appointment, Wesayehu said that the Falashas had been severely oppressed under the imperial regime but that they now had all the rights and privileges given to every other social and ethnic group. "It is only the outside media that create certain distortions and misperceptions," he asserted.

In the late 1970s, Yehuda and a few other Israeli Falashas had been recruited by the Jewish Agency and another organization to try to smuggle Ethiopian Jews out across the Kenyan border. But at the time, they were an inexperienced and inept team, and one attempt ended in disaster—a truckload of Falashas from Ambover were caught and imprisoned. The ill-planned effort was paid for by the Jewish Agency. The agency also hired a pair of Frenchmen to bring Ethiopian Jews to Kenya at the rate of five hundred dollars a head, but they only succeeded in getting more people arrested.

Later, when a route to Sudan opened up, many other groups would be caught, jailed, and tortured. After several months in prison, most of them were released if they signed documents stating that if they were caught a second time trying to flee the country, they would be sentenced to death. They signed, but most of them set out again on the journey, an epic march out of Ethiopia.

4

Crossroads Sudan

To some of his supporters, Menachem Begin was "The Commander," the century's greatest Jewish nationalist, an eloquent and tough king of Israel. To his foes, he was a cynical politician, a hypocrite and deceiver who could tolerate only yes-men around him. Ze'ev Jabotinsky, the secularist founder of the nationalist movement Begin headed for so many years, must have turned in his grave whenever Begin donned a skullcap and intoned *Baruch Hashem* and *B'ezrat Hashem*—"praise

64

the Lord" and "with the help of God." But whatever else he may have been, the "superhawk" who signed Israel's peace treaty with Egypt was always a true believer in the *essence* of Zionism. There was no cynicism behind his belief in the ingathering of the exiles, black or white, and he fully accepted the task of bringing as many Ethiopian Jews as possible to Israel.

The rescue of the Falashas took a more energetic course because Begin believed that it was a religious imperative to help redeem the black Jews of Africa. Ethiopian Jews who have been associated with the rescue operations call him "the father of our *aliyah.*"

Begin himself has refused to discuss his role in bringing the Falashas to Israel, other than to say that it constitutes a great chapter in Jewish history. He told me once that he was not prepared to speak out until all the Jews of Ethiopia were brought to Israel. But his closest aide, Yehiel Kadishai, has said that at the very beginning of Begin's administration, the prime minister expressed his desire to bring "the Lost Tribe" to Israel because "they are so far away from us and so persecuted and getting fewer and fewer." Begin also said that the color of skin was immaterial—a Jew is a Jew, and a Jew in distress must be helped. Begin would later liken their hazardous exodus from Ethiopia to the *aliyah* of European Jewish refugees.

The man Begin put in charge of "the Falasha question" shortly after he came to power in mid-1977 was his chief military adviser, Brigadier General Ephraim "Froike" Poran, who was closely linked to Israel's security services. For the Beta-Israel, it proved a fortunate coincidence that Poran, the ex–army spokesman and chief military aide to former prime minister Yitzhak Rabin, became the majordomo of the Ethiopian immigration. Poran was an ex-student of Professor Aryeh Tartakower's, expert on the Ten Lost Tribes and Jerusalem representative of the World Jewish Congress. For many years Tartakower headed the Israeli pro-Falasha committee. Poran—like Begin, Tartakower, and Sephardic chief rabbi Ovadia Yosef—also believed that the Falashas were the Lost Tribe of Dan and that Israel must save them.

But when Poran first came into the picture, he was confronted with a quagmire created by the Jewish Agency. Under the 1977 agreement worked out with Mengistu by a Mossad man—call him Nir—two Israel Defense Forces aircraft had brought military shipments to Addis Ababa. The planes had flown back with a total of 121 Ethiopian Jews, including the Falashas' high priest, Uri Ben-Baruch of Wallaca. But four other Israeli air force planes that brought arms to Ethiopia went back empty because of Jewish Agency inefficiency. The main problem was the lack of a coordinator between the Mossad, the agency, the Mengistu government, and the Falashas. There *was* a knowledgeable, experienced Israeli on hand in Ethiopia, a man who had once headed the ORT aid program in Gondar Province and was willing to coordinate operations; but the Jewish Agency, for obscure reasons of its own, vetoed his participation. Nor could Yona Bogala perform the essential task—at that point he was in his seventies and spent much of his time in the north in the Falasha villages. He was also furious about the agency's veto of the capable Israeli, whom he knew and trusted. So a golden opportunity was missed. And then Moshe Dayan's "slip of the tongue" in Geneva in February 1978, when he revealed Israel's arms deal with Ethiopia, effectively put an end to the Falasha *aliyah* for over a year.

But in early 1979, the "Sudan route" opened up in the wake of the insurgencies that were sweeping Ethiopia. The drought and famine that were afflicting wide areas of Africa also contributed to the mass exodus. Hundreds of thousands of Eritrean and Tigrean refugees had trekked to refugee camps in eastern Sudan. A few Falashas would hardly be noticed.

The Sudan route was first suggested to Begin by Yehuda and the other Beta-Israel leaders in Israel at one of their meetings with the prime minister. They had heard that twelve Falashas had gone to Sudan and obtained work there. General Poran sent Nir, the Mossad man, to Khartoum to arrange transport for the twelve Falashas, but he had difficulty finding them. Contact was finally made in a roundabout way. One of the Falashas in the Sudan sent a message to a leader of the American Association for Ethiopian Jews, who passed it on to the Israelis. (Later, some AAEJ people would assert that they had "discovered" the Sudan route and pressed their plan on a reluctant Israeli government. The AAEJ issued a broadside dated November 27, 1985, attacking as inaccurate a book on Operation Moses by Tudor Parfitt. The statement said that in 1979 the AAEJ "felt compelled to act when it became apparent that nothing was being done to get Jews out of Sudan." The AAEJ asserted that it later pulled out its team at the request of the Israelis, but that the Jewish Agency thereafter "ceased operations.")

Soon after the twelve Falashas were taken out of Sudan, the Israelis dispatched some top intelligence

people to Khartoum to appraise the situation and report on the logistical difficulties of a large-scale clandestine *aliyah* movement in an enemy country. Chief
among those Israelis was "B," an aide to Yitzhak
Shamir, Begin's eventual successor. Shamir himself
had spent twenty years in the Mossad and had worked
in Egypt, among other places. His aide was similarly
linked to the security services, as well as to the diplomatic service. Several of the key people involved in
Operation Moses were Foreign Ministry personnel
with Mossad backgrounds. Shortly before leaving
government service, General Poran sent "Joshua" to
Sudan. Joshua, a potbellied middle-aged man, was the
senior operations officer in the Mossad. He would become the man in charge of clandestine operations to
rescue Ethiopian Jews.

As the groundwork was prepared, word soon spread
to Falasha villages—primarily in Wolkait and Tigre—
that there might be a way out. No additional encour-
agement was needed.

In the months after Israel and Egypt began their
historic rapprochement in October 1978, Begin re-
portedly asked President Anwar Sadat to approach
Sudan's president Gaafar Nimeiry about allowing the
Falashas to emigrate from Sudan to Israel by way of
Europe. Nimeiry had been the only Arab leader to
back Sadat and the Camp David peace process. The
Egyptians adamantly refused Begin's request and gave
Nimeiry a full report on the episode. Nevertheless,
Nimeiry would eventually turn a blind eye to the exodus of groups of Falashas, although he feared the
inevitable repercussions in the Arab world if the story
became known.

In 1982 Nimeiry instituted Islamic Law, the *sharia*,

which provided for public hangings and amputations of the limbs of thieves and smugglers. But he still had to fight Moslem fundamentalists led by the Moslem Brotherhood—which he called the Brotherhood of Satan. By 1984 his drought-ravaged country's economy was sinking faster than the Nile, whose waters were at the lowest ebb in living memory. Whatever resources remained were being drained by the festering war against animist and Christian tribes in the equatorial south. Hundreds of thousands of refugees from Ethiopia and Chad were flowing across Sudan's borders. Libya and Ethiopia were interfering in Sudan's internal affairs. Saudi Arabian bankers were milking the country instead of extending aid. In other words, Nimeiry had bigger problems to worry about.

The Israelis worked on their own, without help from Sudan's biggest aid donor, the United States, until the months immediately preceding the Operation Moses airlift. Contacts with Sudanese officials were haphazard.

In the six years of Menachem Begin's administration that ended in 1983, a total of about three thousand Ethiopian Jews would be brought to Israel. But more importantly, Begin set things in motion in the government, paving the way for the much larger influx that was to come.

THE CAUSE OF the Ethiopian Jews attracted a wide variety of personalities, some with perhaps questionable motives, others unquestionably altruistic. From the early days of involvement in the Falasha cause, these included committed Zionists, maverick American officials, do-gooders, highly paid rescuers and idealistic volunteers, starry-eyed intellectuals, Christian friends of Israel, Moslems, the sly and the straight. At several points the Falashas came into conflict with those who believed they represented Falasha interests. An inordinately large number of people would eventually claim responsibility for saving the Ethiopian Jews, including some American government officials, officers of Jewish organizations, publicists, and members of the American Association for Ethiopian Jewry. The Mossad, which did the most, would not talk about its achievement. Not a word.

The small, activist AAEJ was a mixed bag. Its leaders did a great deal of good in stirring interest in the welfare of the Falashas and in pushing for action by the Israelis and by the American government. But there was also cause for censure of their sometimes intemperate propaganda—such as their trumpeting of the fact that thousands of Ethiopian Jews were in Sudan, which was technically in a state of war with Israel. Their own operatives had managed to extract a small number of Falashas out of the Horn of Africa, but Israeli officials said that the amateurs sometimes impeded the big ongoing rescue effort.

But in America at least, the AAEJ people were the only ones to work assiduously on behalf of the Ethiopian Jews, although in 1980 the National Jewish Community Relations Advisory Council also formed a committee on Ethiopian Jews. The establishment Jews had to be goaded constantly; and for years, the AAEJ was all alone in its concern for the Beta-Israel. AAEJ founder Graenum Berger and the group's successive leaders, Professor Howard Lenhoff of California and Nate Shapiro of Illinois, devoted their personal fortunes and years of their lives to rallying support for the Falashas. One AAEJ activist—call him "the Jewish pimpernel"—personally was responsible for saving about two hundred Ethiopian Jews. A young American Jew associated with the AAEJ, Bill Halpern, lost his life on an African road during an attempt to help some Ethiopian Jews in 1979. But one Israeli official said in September 1984, in response to some of the AAEJ's propaganda: "Thousands of Falashas are on the way—the process is on. But it gets blocked up by these self-righteous people who don't care if a thousand are lost, just as long as they can say that they saved a hundred people while Israel did nothing."

Although Menachem Begin had given the matter top priority, he couldn't publicize the fact or answer the AAEJ's allegations of "a conspiracy" of indifference, racism, and neglect. At the annual convention of American Jewish Federations in Detroit in 1980, Begin was heckled by a vociferous group of pro-Falasha activists. Begin kept silent, telling his aides that "once something is out, it will all get out. I will not utter a word that could end this rescue operation."

Some of the most outspoken North American Jews on the Falasha issue were so-called Zionists who professed indignation that the Israelis were not doing more to bring the Ethiopian Jews "home." They held an idealized and naive vision of both Israel and the Falashas. Others, who were more open-minded, acquired expertise in dealing with Israeli and American officials and were not hindered by their own rhetoric.

And what of the Beta-Israel themselves? They never wavered in their belief that they would be redeemed from the centuries in exile. Over the years every visitor to the remote Falasha villages was told on departure: "Do not forget us." The Ethiopian Jews prayed daily that they would be able to see Jerusalem. They risked their lives to get there. Immigration to Israel was *their* idea, and not simply the result of outside effort. They are the ones who willed it.

THE TIMELESS DESERT city of Khartoum is a meeting place of waters and people. It is at the juncture of the Blue Nile and the White Nile, the first flowing swiftly from the Ethiopian highlands where the Falashas have lived for millennia, the latter broad and placid, meandering its way from the lakes of Uganda. Khartoum—at the crossroads of the Arab and African worlds, the place where Islam and Christianity conjoin—was a focal point in the rescue of the Jewish Ethiopians, and Yehuda was among a handful of veteran immigrants sent there from Israel at crucial moments of the operation. His most vital contribution was made during a ten-month period in 1980, when he led small groups of Falashas out of the Sudan and did some of the spadework for the eventual massive immigration of Ethiopian Jews.

Khartoum looks like a giant unfinished project— dusty, dilapidated, funky. The heat is scorching and enervating even in January, the coolest month, with temperatures averaging around ninety degrees. For Yehuda, raised in the cool Ethiopian highlands and grown used to the pleasant high-desert climate of Jerusalem, the heat of the Sudanese capital was unbearable. To avoid the searing sun, Yehuda, like other visitors, would take exorbitantly expensive taxi rides even for the shortest distances. He thought it a won-

der that hundreds of thousands of starving, malnourished refugees, including many of his own people,
were surviving in camps in the much hotter desert
regions far to the east of the capital.

Yehuda's papers—the name he was using and the
nationality—were false. It was a dangerous assign-
ment, and he was risking his life. (It wasn't until the
summer of 1984 that the Sudanese secret service
would cooperate with Israel through the Americans,
who were acting on Jerusalem's behalf.) Yehuda's
immediate predecessor as the Falasha coordinator of
an immigration effort that was just getting off the
ground in 1980 was a Tigrean Falasha. But he was
arrested soon after his arrival, and getting him freed
was a complicated affair. The Tigrean Jew had had
no guidelines or training for this special task. Yehuda also was not a trained intelligence agent. Although he had often been called on to do such work
since 1977, he knew his limitations. But he had also
learned a great deal "on the job," including the les-
sons of earlier failed rescue missions.

He felt at ease in Khartoum's dusty streets jammed
with people of various colors and costumes. He found
that the atmosphere was usually relaxed, and the
Sudanese he encountered were generally friendly,
warm, and helpful, including a high official who arranged a visa—in exchange for generous *baksheesh*.
But Yehuda usually kept to himself and met only the
people he had to meet.

On one occasion, he was walking through a street
toward his hotel, the seedy Acropole in the center of
town, when someone called him by his name. He ignored the man, an Ethiopian Jew who had known
Yehuda in Addis Ababa. The man immediately real-

ized his blunder and melted into the crowd. He and Yehuda would laugh about it years later, when they met again at Ben-Gurion Airport. On another occasion, he was arrested briefly by a man who searched his valise, found $250 in it, and said, "You stole this." Under questioning, Yehuda told the man that he was an Ethiopian political refugee, a teacher, and that the money came from a cousin in Italy. In the time-honored tradition, he reached an "agreement" with the man, giving him all but a few of the dollars. Yehuda had another $2,000 in his shoes. He had concealed much larger sums of money at various locations in Khartoum and in the eastern town of Gedaref, the hub of the refugee area.

A few thousand Falashas had reached the refugee camps by the spring of 1980, and Yehuda, after conferring with Israeli agents who had flown in from Nairobi or entered Sudan through Juba in the south, immediately made contact with his people. He told them that small groups, ranging from fifteen to forty people, would be taken out of the camps every week or so by bus, truck, or Land-Rover. They might spend some time in Gedaref before traveling on to Khartoum, where they would stay in a safe house until they could be flown out to Athens or Paris.

Within two months of his arrival, Yehuda had helped the Mossad to build up a network of people that arranged for internal travel permits from the Interior Ministry and the police, and documents from the Red Cross and Sudanese refugee officials. These documents were easily altered—photographs switched to include whole families, names added above the proper stamps. But securing a safe house in Khartoum proved a difficult problem; it was hard to find a place where a few dozen Ethiopian refugees would go unnoticed. Besides, the rental-housing market in Khartoum was extremely limited. But finally, with the help of an Eritrean woman who ran a call-girl operation and was well connected, Yehuda rented a large house next door to a brothel.

At times fifty or sixty Falashas were staying at the house for up to a month. With so many people living cooped up together it was impossible to maintain the desired low profile. On several occasions, neighbors—including the prostitutes—complained to the police about the large number of Ethiopians living in the house. Yehuda always managed to smooth things over. But it was soon necessary to find another safe house—a compound that was much more private.

Yehuda himself switched hotels constantly. Once he stayed at the luxurious, Chinese-built Friendship Palace Hotel; at other times he lived in malarial flea-bags where the sewage flowed in the halls. His meetings with the Mossad men took place in cars or restaurants. Great sums of money were transferred in grocery bags. Every two weeks he received ninety thousand Sudanese pounds (then about twenty thousand dollars), which he brought to the refugee camps. The three thousand Jews in the camps and in the town of Gedaref had organized themselves and appointed steering committees of five persons, who dispensed the money that Yehuda brought them.

But the money created as many problems as it solved. Heated, ugly arguments arose over the amounts distributed to single persons, couples, families. It also stirred the suspicions of the Falashas' fellow refugees and of Sudanese personnel in and around the camps.

The biggest disagreements, however, were over who was to go and when. Everyone wanted to be first, creating a constant conflict between the steering committees and the refugees. A couple of the Falasha list makers took advantage of their position and sought bribes or sexual favors.

It took many months to work out a successful transport system. Sudan was plagued by a severe fuel shortage, and gas had to be bought on the black market at astronomical prices. Even President Nimeiry, on a plane trip to Juba, in Equatoria, had to bring enough fuel for the return trip, since none was available in Sudan's second largest city. It cost about a thousand dollars just to rent a Land-Rover for a couple of days, and it took at least five hours to get from the capital to Gedaref on a road paved two-thirds of the way. The drivers were paid "per head" upon successful delivery in Khartoum. They always traveled at night in order to arrive back in Khartoum before dawn, when few people would be around to witness the unloading of refugees at the safe house. The police and army roadblocks at various points along the route were not a problem. In a world where bribery is a way of life, there were few arrests or delays that could not be finessed.

On one occasion, Yehuda had to carry a sick, raving old man into the house, assuring him that he was on his way to Israel. But a Mossad agent who was in the house told Yehuda that he should send the man back to the refugee camp, that he was obviously too ill to take to the airport, and that it might somehow torpedo the entire operation. Yehuda fed the man some rice, then turned to the Mossad agent and said, "I'll take care of him. He'll die otherwise." Yehuda threatened to quit if the Mossad man got his way. For the next two weeks, Yehuda fed and cared for the old man, until he could walk with a cane. A year later, the two met again, at an absorption center in Israel.

Yehuda admired the Mossad people for their professionalism, self-confidence, soldierliness. Nir, the man who had negotiated with Ethiopia's Mengistu and who had spirited the first Falashas out of Sudan, was different from the other Mossadniks in Sudan— a wild, daring type, an actor and the most effective agent. He was a natural when meticulously dressed in suit and tie and negotiating a contract or when playing the dusty vagabond toting a backpack and walking down the road. During a weekly run from the refugee camps, one of two Land-Rovers broke down. The tow chain had inadvertently been left back in Khartoum. Nir walked ten miles to Gedaref, climbed the wall of a church, and expropriated the chain from the church's bell. "The Vatican owes it to the Jews," he figured.

Several of the Mossadniks spoke fluent Sudanese Arabic. All of them had excellent cover. They supervised most aspects of the operation and acted as "firemen" whenever necessary. On one occasion, some of the Jewish refugees were mistakenly placed on a Saudi Arabian airliner and had to be discreetly pulled off.

The travel and technical arrangements for the groups of Falashas flown out of Sudan were made by a front organization set up for the operation, with offices in Europe and Africa. The refugees—usually in groups of fifteen or thirty and never exceeding sixty— were flown to Athens on Olympic Airways, and from Athens to Israel by Olympic or El Al. They were always accompanied by Yehuda or another Israeli Falasha, as well as by other Jews. Athens was the closest

European city to Israel, and it was imperative to move them as quickly as possible for security reasons and to enable them to get badly needed medical treatment. Yehuda would then fly back to Sudan via Europe.

According to some reports, the Sudan office of the United Nations High Commissioner for Refugees also played a role in facilitating the exit of the Jews through the granting of group visas, but an Israeli intelligence source denies that the UNHCR cooperated in any way. "They didn't want to be accused of helping out only the Jews, which was legitimate from their point of view. So we avoided them." But several Falashas who were imprisoned for leaving the camps without authorization reportedly were helped by a French UNHCR official in Gedaref, Jean-Claude Concolato, who sympathized with their plight.

One of the Falashas who was taken out of Khartoum via the route that Yehuda helped to set up later recalled his two months of complete seclusion in a safe house. "We were hidden. We did what we were told to do. We asked no questions. We knew that we were in the hands of our brothers and that they were leading us to freedom."

He and the other thirty-three people in his group had no idea where they were when they reached Athens. "We got to some airport where a white woman met us. They examined us with machines, and then we were taken to rest. Afterwards, our group boarded another plane. The rest of the passengers were white people. We warned the children not to eat the food, that it wasn't kosher. When we arrived in Israel, we were told that we had arrived home. We were overcome with joy."

After leading scores of other Ethiopian Jews to Israel during his nearly one year in Sudan, Yehuda was relieved by another veteran Israeli Falasha. Afterward, Yehuda never spent more than a few days at a time in Sudan, although they were usually at crucial moments. Eventually, he would see the dreams of thousands of his people fulfilled.

IT WAS NOT increasing persecution or the famine alone that spurred the exodus of the Falashas. The longing to go to Israel began to reach fever pitch because of the news that hundreds of Falashas were managing to get there. Occasional visitors to the Falasha villages in northwest Ethiopia, including some Israeli Falashas like Yehuda, helped to accelerate the movement. Of course it would probably be correct to say that almost everybody in impoverished, brutal, drought-struck Ethiopia, Jewish or not, would have grabbed a chance to go to a country like Israel. But the Falashas were driven by an added factor: they believed that God was telling them, "This is the time."

Parts of the terrain through which the Jews walked from Ethiopia to Sudan is among the most spectacular on earth. Some of the plateaus are set among a maze of razor-sharp ridges, with sudden plunges thousands of feet into lush, dark gorges and valleys cut by swift rivers and dotted with purple-and-pink irises, baobab, and mimosa trees. In their grueling trek, the Falashas also traversed great tracts of flat desert land that had been stripped of its sparse vegetation. No islands of shade remained beneath the acacia trees, because the leaves had been consumed by starving peasants and the branches had been cut for fuel.

Early in 1980, Yehuda managed to send word to his sixty-year-old brother, Avraham, who lived in a village near Ambover in Gondar Province, that a few hundred Jews from the Tigre and Aramcheho regions were getting to Israel via Sudan. Gondar was much farther away, and the danger of being caught was greater. Avraham and his cousin Yehoshua, a learned, "political" man who had welcomed the Marxist revolution, were told by a local guide that it would be simple. Rather than attempt to cross the jungles of Aramcheho, they, their families, and their neighbors could go to Gondar town, a day's walk away, where they could get a bus to Metemma near the Sudan border. But the plan ended in disaster. In Metemma, the seventy-three people in the group were caught by soldiers. Avraham, Yehoshua, and the other heads of households were flown by helicopter to the prison in Gondar. Most of the remaining people were marched from Metemma to Gondar, a two-week ordeal during which several died.

Avraham and Yehoshua spent seven months in a large cell with 120 other prisoners. Each inmate had about one square yard of room in which to live. Their only exercise was to dig graves for the many who died of disease or who were executed or beaten to death. A car came every day to take people away to be shot. Altogether, over 500 Jews from Gondar, Tigre, and Wolkait were in the prison. But the Jews were not singled out for execution. At least in this matter, the revolutionary regime adhered to its ideology of equality for the minorities. But there was continual fear among the prisoners, who waited every day to see who would be beaten or executed.

According to Yehoshua, a sixty-five-year-old man with eleven children, "Immediately after the revolution, the lives of Ethiopian Jews improved. There was equality under the Dergue. Even when the local people continued subjugating us, the regime tried to bring about equality." But the authorities started to crack down on the Falashas when it became clear that they were determined to leave for Israel. "Thereafter they actively persecuted Jews by limiting freedom of religious expression to Christians and Moslems only. Every Shabbat, we were subjected to brainwashing sessions. The Jews realized that they were being told to 'worship' the new regime instead of Elohim. They were not taken in by the fictions of Marxism. But the regime was attempting to undermine our traditions, to discredit the family unit. They encouraged our children to break away from the tradition. We could not tolerate that."

The authorities wanted to know which men were responsible for planning the journey to Sudan. The guards hanged Yehoshua by his feet and beat his testicles. "I lost count of time." In a separate chamber, Avraham's hands and feet were bound around a two-by-four piece of lumber. The guards turned him upside down and beat his legs with cudgels. At one point, three torturers worked simultaneously, beating his hands and feet bloody until they tired from physical strain. Avraham broke under the torture and admitted that it was all the guide's idea.

The guide, Avraham, and Yehoshua were placed in solitary confinement for a few days, then put in the same room to be tortured together. "It was a miracle I was not crippled," Avraham recalled. "Many others were. They beat the flesh off an Ambover teacher's legs—right down to the bone. Then they gave him shots so he wouldn't die from the worms."

After seven months Avraham's name was called; he

was to be released. He was brought before provincial governor Malaku, who warned him, "Your life is in your hands. You'll die if you are caught again." For the next three years, Avraham was obsessed with escaping from Ethiopia. When the big push finally came in 1984, he would be among the leaders.

Yehoshua and his family were held for eleven months. "They kept asking us why we wanted to leave the country after we had been granted equal rights. I was singled out along with one of our religious leaders and charged with being a leader of the *aliyah* movement. We continued to be tortured mercilessly. They couldn't understand it. They'd ask, 'You still want to go to Israel?' They said that we were black and Israelis were white and that we couldn't become white. I answered that *aliyah* isn't a matter of color, that Jews all over the world look like their neighbors."

One of the interrogators accused him of being among the "Zionist agents" instigating the people to leave and said that it might be best "to destroy you." Yehoshua replied, "You may destroy my physical being, but you can't destroy my soul." Yehoshua explained later, "These brave words were not my own invention. In the last century, Emperor Theodore threatened to mutilate a Falasha holy man, the monk Abba Simon, who refused to be baptized and insisted on the unity of God as against the trinity. It was like the Marxists trying to impose their religion on us. Abba Simon told the king, 'You can cut and split my flesh, but you cannot touch my soul.' That encounter over a hundred years ago is what set off the movement to walk to Zion."

Yehoshua said that his interrogator "tried to prove

that I was an Ethiopian and not a Jew. I said that throughout our history in Ethiopia we were strangers in the land, hungering to return to Zion—our history proves it."

The brainwashing didn't work, and Yehoshua and his family were released "because it was the will of God."

IN 1981, A YEAR after Yehuda had helped to launch the "underground railroad" through Sudan, about six hundred Falashas were brought out of Khartoum by the Mossad operation. In 1982 and 1983, the total figure jumped to about three thousand, as Falashas were taken out along two new routes in addition to the Khartoum passage. Some of these refugees were brought by ship from Port Sudan to Israel's Red Sea port at Eilat. In the months it took to prepare this route, the Mossad and frogmen from the Israeli navy charted the entire harbor area of Port Sudan so that there would be no accidents around the dangerous reefs. The refugees were brought out on a total of nineteen Israeli naval vessels, including Dabur missile boats, beach-landing craft, and a special U.S.-built speedboat that could carry up to forty passengers. Some Falashas were brought out by submarine.

Every sector of the Israel Defense Forces was involved, and, as one participant put it, "It was the cream of the crop—the elite commando units, communications men, pilots, frogmen." The Ethiopian Jews were taken by truck or bus to a relatively secluded part of the port directly from a rendezvous a few miles outside the Tuwawa refugee camp, about four hundred miles away. The biggest group numbered 350.

The operation was conducted without the cooperation of Sudanese officials or the secret police. In fact, several suspected Falasha agents were imprisoned by the Sudanese between 1980 and 1984. The Sudanese had no idea of the extent of the Mossad operation, although they knew something was going on. To aid in surveillance, the Mossad brazenly opened a business in one strategic location. President Nimeiry continued to ignore the fact that Jews were being taken out of his country to Israel.

The Red Sea route came to an abrupt and bloody end in early March 1982 as eleven Dabur boats waited offshore to collect twenty passengers each. Two Mossad agents and an Israeli Falasha were unloading three truckloads of refugees when a group of Sudanese soldiers appeared suddenly. The refugees all broke into a frantic run, but several were caught. One of the Falashas was wounded when the soldiers opened fire. The Israelis returned the fire and the soldiers fled. The incident, in which there were several casualties, never appeared in the press or was picked up by the diplomatic grapevine in Khartoum. But that was it for Port Sudan.

The Mossad had completed contingency planning for an alternative route if something went wrong at Port Sudan. In any case it was known that the numbers that could be brought out via the original Khartoum route could never exceed more than sixty a week without endangering the whole operation, and that was not fast enough.

In the early evening of March 16, 1982, an unmarked Israel Defense Forces C-130 Hercules transport plane landed in the dusty, barren scrubland about twenty miles from Doka, exactly midway be-

tween the two refugee camps where most of the Falashas were located: Tuwawa and Umm Rekuba. The
plane was supposed to take on about one hundred
Falashas, but close to a thousand showed up. The "list
makers" in the camps had gone about their business
too far in advance of the flight. Everyone knew about
it, and no one wanted to be left behind. The frenzied
refugees swamped the plane and couldn't be beaten
off with wooden staves. The pilot, viewing the panic,
decided to take off when the plane was only half full.
In the ensuing confusion, an overcrowded truck carrying disappointed refugees back to the camp over-
turned, injuring many of the passengers.

The "Gedaref route" was off to an inauspicious start.
In addition to the Mossad's problem of reorganizing
the refugees to prevent a recurrence of such pandemonium, it was obvious that the desert landings
might easily be discovered by the Sudanese army. So
it was decided to use the route sparingly, even though
the rate of the exodus from Ethiopia was beginning
to mushroom. Over the next twenty-five months, six
Hercules operations took place involving nine planes.

During the later actions, there generally was less
panic among the refugees. They were informed that
they were to go only three hours before the flights.
On one occasion, three planes took part in the action, on another, two planes. Altogether about thirteen hundred Falashas were flown directly to Israel
in the Mossad's desert operation.

All nine Hercules planes carried medical teams as
well as commando units of eighteen men, who fanned
out in squads of three to protect the refugees and their
rescuers. In the six operations, the Israelis never had
occasion to open fire.

Yehuda and two other Israeli Falashas took part in
all of the Hercules operations, translating and helping care for the refugees. Many of the Ethiopian Jews
were suffering from disease—in one case, Sudan's
dreaded "green monkey fever." The highly conta-
gious brain disease, or something akin to it, was di-
agnosed in a delirious boy within hours of his arrival
at Tel Hashomer Hospital in Tel Aviv. The alarm went
out. All the refugees who had arrived in Israel that
morning and been dispersed to reception centers
throughout the country had to be rounded up, as well
as the plane crew and the commandoes. Yehuda and
the medical team who had tended the boy during the
flight were vaccinated and put in quarantine for a
week. That no one else contracted the disease, and
that the boy eventually recovered, was something of
a medical miracle.

In March 1984, nomadic Sudanese camel herders
camping in a dry riverbed near the desert airstrip saw
two of the planes take off and reported the incident
to the authorities. Rumors soon swept diplomatic and
intelligence circles in Khartoum. Everyone knew it
had something to do with the Ethiopian Jews. But no
one got the story exactly straight. Western diplomats
later told reporters that they believed there had been
only one such flight, other sources said that there had
been four.

As the number of Falasha refugees swelled, the
Mossad had planned to bring four Hercules planes
twice a week, but now it looked to be too risky. The
planes wouldn't be caught by the Sudanese radar in
Gedaref or Port Sudan—the soldiers who operated the
radar were asleep most of the time, according to
Mossad agents. But the Bedouin were a major prob-

lem: they might bring the secret police and the army. Hundreds of Ethiopian Jews could be killed or the pipeline cut off entirely.

What turned out to be the last of the flights, on May 4, 1984, went unnoticed by the nomads, the Sudan secret police, and the diplomats alike. But it was a close call nevertheless. Mossad agents drove the trucks to the site and the refugees climbed down. As soon as the refugees saw the plane land, though, they panicked as before and ran in all directions. It took hours to round the Falashas up, and the organizers of the operation could find no trace of one elderly woman. They left without her. Sudanese soldiers found her a day later wandering around in the middle of nowhere. They wanted to know how she had gotten there. She said she didn't know. They assumed she was suffering from sunstroke and drove her to a clinic in Gedaref. Fortunately, the Sudanese did not question her further. But the risks remained. Later several Falasha refugees were arrested outside Tuwawa. No one could be sure that they wouldn't talk under torture. The Khartoum rumor mill was buzzing. It was too dangerous to continue the flights. When they were canceled for security reasons, the stage was set for the Mossad to turn to the Americans.

IN NEIGHBORING ETHIOPIA, Colonel Mengistu was not cooperating in any way, according to Israeli sources who vigorously deny that any deal was struck with Addis Ababa. But one informed Jewish U.S. government official told me in Washington that Ethiopia "got a lot of goodies from both Israel and the United States for turning a blind eye to the exit of the Jews. Much of the military hardware and communications systems in Ethiopia are Israeli." It is known that Israel sent some $20 million worth of small arms and equipment to Addis Ababa in 1983.

When the U.S. official approached Colonel Mengistu about the Ethiopian Jews in mid-1980, the Ethiopian dictator said that he would never forgive Moshe Dayan's 1978 "treachery." He added that he would not cooperate in the emigration of Ethiopian Jews because he was under pressure from the Soviet bloc as well as from the Arabs and the Organization of African Unity.

Meanwhile, the AAEJ was continuing its campaign of recriminations against the Israeli government. In 1982 an AAEJ leader asserted that Jewish Agency immigration official Yehuda Dominitz and the Foreign Ministry's official in charge of "diaspora affairs," Moshe Gilboa, had been "sabotaging" any significant movement of Falashas to Israel. Although Dominitz had definitely opposed Falasha immigration in the early 1970s, there was no evidence a decade later that he actively impeded rescue efforts. Quite the contrary. In any case, it was completely in the hands of the Mossad. And Gilboa had no power whatsoever. However, the AAEJ effort to keep up the pressure was probably a good idea, even though Israel had shown that it was now thoroughly committed to helping the Ethiopian Jews and that there was no going back. And at the same time, the AAEJ continued to enlist U.S. legislators to push for Falasha immigration to Israel.

But the group's often self-congratulatory publicity campaign brought injurious media attention to the continuing major efforts by the Mossad when sensitive information appeared in the *Miami Herald* at the

end of 1981. Then in mid-July 1983, after members
of an AAEJ rescue mission and several Falashas were
arrested in Juba, Sudan, one hundred miles from the
Kenyan border, the *Nairobi Standard* picked up the
story, including details of the "underground railroad" taking Ethiopian Jews out of Sudan and
through Kenya. Nir, the Mossad agent, had warned
the American-Jewish group that the Juba route was
too dangerous—the Mossad itself had rejected it. But
the AAEJ "knew better." Now, with U.S. diplomatic
help, the AAEJ was able to extricate the arrested
Americans and their Falasha charges. The AAEJ
"pimpernel" had had only the best of intentions and
stopped once he understood that he might endanger
the major Mossad effort. (The AAEJ's statement of
November 27, 1985, said that the AAEJ mission had
brought out 129 Falashas "through the swamps of
Sudan during the summer, although Jewish organizations had been told for three years that rains made
summer rescues impossible. In late 1983, an agreement was reached that AAEJ would pull out of
Sudan and that Mossad would clean out the camps.
All Jews in Sudan at that time—some 3,000—were
brought into Israel. The fact that this number was
rescued following the AAEJ mission clearly indicates
that the charge that AAEJ 'blocked' rescues is un-
founded." Although it was true that no Mossad missions were canceled because of the AAEJ, the group's
foul-ups definitely threatened the whole project, according to Israeli officials.) The AAEJ's activities and
its references to Sudan also led to a July 1983 article
in the London *Observer* that almost put an end to the
entire operation: "An underground network is chan-
nelling the Falashas . . . out of their homeland to

become settlers in Israel. The network is largely financed by Jewish pressure groups in the United States and Canada. The operation is being conducted in the greatest secrecy because the Falashas' only escape route is through the Sudan, an Islamic country. . . . A key role in this has been played by the American Association for Ethiopian Jews, founded by Graenum Berger."

Several journalists familiar with the Falasha story, as well as "neutral observers," have stated that the AAEJ "did very much more harm than good," in the words of British professor Tudor Parfitt, who reported on the Falasha immigration for the London-based Minority Rights Group. However, this assessment is still open to question, for only the AAEJ was warning in 1983 that thousands of Jews were facing death by disease and starvation in the refugee camps of Sudan. In early September 1984 Berger said, "We know hundreds are dying now. Israel could get them out." Even in their negative activities, the AAEJ seemed to serve as a catalyst, causing Israel to accelerate its efforts to save the Ethiopian Jews.

But even as Operation Moses was about to be launched, Berger—who had been told by a State Department official about the airlift plan but who reportedly believed that it was just another Israeli trick—was writing to newspapers about the Jews in the camps, specifically mentioning Sudan. Any mention of Sudan was rigorously censored in the Israeli press, but American Jewish newspapers, working without any guidelines, did not delete Berger's indiscreet remarks. Later, in the midst of Operation Moses, a few AAEJ members would continue the war of words over the Ethiopian rescue. In a letter to the *Seattle*

Times on January 31, 1985, the association's local
representative repeated the AAEJ's 1982 charge concerning Moshe Gilboa and others and said that he had
been told "by several reliable sources" that certain
Israeli officials had "sabotaged and managed to temporarily halt the evacuation of Ethiopian Jews from
the Sudan at the end of last May." The AAEJ's rhetoric had obviously not changed with the times.

The actions of the AAEJ's counterpart organization, the Canadian Association for Ethiopian Jews,
were also criticized as "reckless and incompetent,"
in the words of one Canadian newsman who accompanied a group of CAEJ members to Ethiopia. Their
efforts failed, and they were thrown out of Ethiopia
by government authorities.

One State Department official, who had tried to
calm down the American association's more vocal
elements who were "talking too much" in the days
leading up to Operation Moses, told me that "the
AAEJ people suffered from overzealousness, but the
airlift would not have happened without them." He
was sharply critical of the Jewish establishment organizations. "NACJRAC, the national body of U.S.
Jewish community councils, was an unabashed tool
of the Israeli government, discrediting the AAEJ and
insisting—when it wasn't true—that Israel was doing
everything possible."

The AAEJ accomplished a great deal, he said, but
it did not give sufficient credit to the Israeli government; and its shrill polemics undermined the importance of the group's more affirmative work. "They
cried wolf too many times. When the wolf was really
at the door and thousands of Falashas were dying,
their warnings simply did not have much effect any-

more." The most important AAEJ contribution, he said, was made in the early 1980s. "The American group realized a new approach was needed, and Nate Shapiro led the way. They went after young congressmen and government aides like Tom Lantos, Steve Solarz, and Ted Weiss and soon developed a cadre of people on Capitol Hill who were interested." Other U.S. congressmen who became involved included Congressman Gary Ackerman of New York, Senator Rudy Boschwitz of Minnesota, and Senator Charles Percy of Illinois. "The mobilizing of U.S. officials is what started the ball rolling. The American congressmen put the pressure on the State Department, and this in turn is what put the pressure on the Israelis to meet the challenge. There was no high-level approach by Israel to the State Department until August 1984. That was months after people around here had been energized."

But a second State Department official, who was much more closely involved in initiating Operation Moses, had a different assessment. "The involvement of the U.S. government had absolutely nothing to do with the AAEJ's efforts. The AAEJ may have done important work years ago in arousing public opinion, but one of their foul-ups—the Juba incident—threatened the entire rescue effort. It's true that they saved some people, and that's just great. But they were blind to the harm they were doing to the big operation. The Sudan government was in great difficulty and was very sensitive. Their disruptiveness in Sudan was absolutely horrendous. But Shapiro at least listened to reason and contributed something to this whole effort."

An official of an establishment American Jewish

organization who followed the activities of the AAEJ believes that despite the sometimes destructive moves by some of the group's members and "an inordinate amount of egotism and overacting," the AAEJ as a whole deserves "a lot" of credit.

But he does not believe that the AAEJ influenced the Israeli government to act. "The AAEJ claimed that only when its ads appeared in the U.S. press did Israel do anything. This is patently untrue. In May 1983 the AAEJ rescued 120 people, and one of the group's leaders, Howard Lenhoff, wrote that 'Israel hardly rescued anyone until we showed the way.' But in the six months from November 1982 to May 1983, the Israelis brought 2,000 Ethiopian Jews to the country. The AAEJ leaders simply misrepresented things and in fact caused operations to be postponed."

The fact was that the Mossad was quietly bringing out about 6,000 Ethiopian Jews in three years, while the AAEJ brought out fewer than 200—"perhaps at the expense of hundreds of others," the Jewish official said. But he acknowledged that the AAEJ's "pimpernel" had often performed courageously. The pimpernel himself wished only to emphasize the positive side. "Great good deeds have been done," he said. "What's the use of dwelling on the mudslinging and bitter recriminations of the past?"

He denied that his activities ever interfered with the Israeli operations. "Any time we were in conflict, we left the area. We made mistakes, but our people did a marvelous job getting people out, and volunteered to go back."

One elderly West Coast couple who split off from the AAEJ because of what they called "their anti-Israel polemics and their general methods" themselves brought over 40 Falashas out of Ethiopia—in ways that cannot be revealed. They worked anonymously, not seeking any publicity or thanks.

BY JANUARY 1984, the refugee camps had been virtually emptied of Jews; only ninety Falashas were left. The Mossad operatives had performed brilliantly. But then came the flood, and the Mossad would no longer be able to handle it alone.

The Ethiopian Jews of Tigre Province and Wolkait were all in Israel now. But the major Beta-Israel population remained behind in Ethiopia, in the Gondar and Woggera areas. In Israel Yehuda was instructed to choose an Israeli Falasha whose word would be respected in these regions, a messenger to tell the people to pick up and leave, to go to Sudan despite the high death rate in the camps. He picked his cousin Dani, who he felt sure would be able to get past the Ethiopian authorities, though the central government was still keeping most visitors out of the Beta-Israel areas. In addition, Dani's family was widely known, the people would listen to him, as they had listened to Yehuda.

In February and March of 1984, Dani brought the message from Israel to the Ethiopian highlands. Word swept through the Falasha villages that the "hour of redemption" was at hand. Once Major Malaku was removed as governor in 1983, it had become easier for the Jews to get out. Malaku had issued a declaration that any Falasha who was caught on his way toward Sudan would be imprisoned and his property confiscated. But his successor rescinded the order, saying that it was not illegal for the Beta-Israel to travel to the west so long as they did not cross the border.

At the same time, the army began a conscription campaign, drafting all able-bodied young men from age sixteen up. In the midst of the worsening famine and stepped-up warfare between the Ethiopian army and Tigrean insurgents, some ten thousand Jews set out for Sudan over a period of about six months. Eight thousand to ten thousand Beta-Israel remained in Ethiopia, mostly the aged, infirm, very small children, and conscripted soldiers who were sent to the distant Somalia front. No young men were left in the Beta-Israel villages.

By the time reports started to come in of the rapidly deteriorating situation in the grim Sudanese refugee camps, where disease was rampant in the summer of 1984, it was too late to stem the tide or to stop the long march altogether. It soon became clear to everyone concerned that the Mossad's apparatus could not rescue such large numbers quickly. Drastic action would have to be taken.

"THE WORD PASSED from person to person, family to family, village to village. Even the sick and old and weak who had no chance of surviving knew that the moment of redemption had arrived," said Yosef of Imphraz village, which is set in rugged, mountainous terrain two days' walk from Gondar. "They heard that if they got to Sudan, they would get to Jerusalem. They sold what they could and gave away the rest to their neighbors and just left."

Yosef, an illiterate farmer and weaver, had heard stories about Jerusalem and the Holy Land from his grandparents, his parents, and the Falasha priests. "They all said that Jerusalem, Zion, is where we came from and where we have to return." The time finally came, in the spring of 1984.

Yosef, who guesses that his age is somewhere between fifty-six and sixty-seven, said that everyone
wanted to make the escape attempt, although they
had no guarantee of success. There would be those
who would make it and those who wouldn't, he said.
They knew they faced attacks and other dangers along
the way, "but nothing else mattered except the goal
of getting to Jerusalem."

He knew that Israel existed. He had visited the large
elementary school in Ambover years before and had
been told that there were white Jews in the world.
Yosef had never heard of any Israeli or Jewish leaders.

In early April 1984 the people of his village gathered at a meeting in their synagogue and decided that
they should try to reach Israel. Their priests recited
the story of the Exodus, psalms lamenting the exile,
and prayers praising the Lord: "There is no one except you." The priests leaned on their wooden prayer
staves and led a rhythmic dance to the accompani-
ment of a small kettledrum, a circular gong, and a
one-string violin. "Show us the light of your praise,
Lord, deliver us because of your name and redeem
us."

Yosef told the local authorities that he was leaving
the area with his wife and four children because his
wife needed medical treatment. The Marxist regime
had recently eased its persecution of the Falashas,
although the Jews were still restricted in practicing
their religion or teaching Hebrew. Yosef had no difficulty in getting permission to sell his cattle and
grain. He also obtained travel passes from the local
peasant association. (Anyone found without a pass was
liable to imprisonment, but most of the Beta-Israel
ignored this stricture.)

Yosef and his family of six left with a group of about

fifty other people. They had mules to carry the children and donkeys to take the supplies, such as flour, coffee, and water in gourds and jerry cans. They had a non-Jewish guide, an apostate Jew who, although he had converted to Christianity, still retained connections with Jewish members of his family.

Yosef's group violated the Sabbath by traveling and by crossing rivers on the day of rest, "but we had to keep going." They started out at an elevation of about fifteen thousand feet above sea level, where the air was thin and cold and the vegetation consisted of lichens and heather. They climbed heights that rose thousands of feet above a dark belt of damp ravines, then descended into broad green pastures. At night, they heard the howling of hyenas; one morning, they sighted a leopard roaming through a grove of kosso trees.

They walked for two days to Ateguy, where they were caught by civil guards. The guide escaped into the bush. These local militiamen, who wore half uniforms of denim shorts, khaki camouflage shirts, and boxy army caps, poked at the Falashas with their Soviet-made automatic rifles. The Jews had to pay a fortune for their freedom. The heads of households negotiated bribes of six hundred birr, or about three hundred dollars, with the local militiamen, who then let them go. The sum involved was the equivalent of more than two years' wages.

The group continued on for three days to a place called Jenda. From Jenda to the Sudan border took them another thirteen days. During this time, they were robbed by a band of *shiftas*, a dozen men on horseback who took most of their animals but left them their meager flour and water supplies.

When the group neared Sudan, the terrain changed

dramatically, as did the climate. They passed castellated rocks that soared out of the flat, stony semiarid region below the foothills. Except for what was offered by a few thorny acacia trees, no more shade was to be found. At a river along the Sudan-Ethiopia border they met some local Ethiopians who warned them of the police and army patrols on both sides of the border and said that they might not be allowed to cross. And even if they could escape the guards, the Falashas were told, they would be trapped in the desert.

The group still had one mule and a little money that had not been given as bribes or stolen. They offered this to the local Ethiopians, who accepted. "We had very little left. But they took pity on us and said they would guide us," Yosef said.

On the route into Sudan, they saw mutilated human and animal corpses everywhere, dried-out cadavers that had been ripped apart by man and hyena. Broad-winged bald buzzards hopped around the bodies, tearing off pieces of flesh.

It took them all night and the next day before they reached an area near Techa. A Sudanese patrol stopped them and detained them for questioning. In most instances, the escaping Falashas were afraid to tell anyone that they were Jews, and it was usually the wisest course. Yosef's group, however, decided differently.

"We saw other Jews there whom we recognized. They had told the Sudanese that they were Christians, whereupon the Moslem guards beat them mercilessly. So our group admitted that we were Jews, who were running away from the regime for political reasons, not because of religious reasons. And they left us alone."

That night they were transported by Sudanese trucks to the Umm Rekuba camp near Gedaref, where most of the Falashas were concentrated among the teeming refugees. Yosef noted that both at Techa and at Umm Rekuba "so many Jews were there I couldn't count them."

Once at Umm Rekuba, Yosef's group conformed to the usual rule and told the authorities that they were Christians. For the first month Yosef's family lived in a small tent and then were moved into one of the round thatched huts of the long-established camp.

Two weeks after their arrival in early summer, children started to die from diarrhea and dehydration. "So many people died then, in the summer heat. So many died and so many were sick that we had no strength left to bury the dead. Some of the huts were filled up with dead people and closed off." The stench of the bloated, blackened bodies was overwhelming.

The death toll among the Jewish refugees rose to about one hundred a week. Bodies were left to rot in the sun. Yosef said that the Red Cross at one point did come and "tried to clear up some of the mess. But the flour provided by the relief workers was wormy, and people got no medical treatment whatsoever."

Yosef told how his wife, Rachel, had taken sick and how he had attended her as she lay dying. They had been married when she was seven, and she was brought up by his family until the marriage could be consummated. "So she was wife, mother, sister, and child to me. But it was God's will. Because she was so beloved. God loved her and took her from us. Today I try to understand why God punished us by taking her, but this is the price that had to be paid for our redemption."

Soon after his wife's death, a brother, several nephews and nieces, and other relatives "beyond count" died of typhus or measles. He lost track of time and place. "I can't describe the horror; I dream about it all the time."

Yosef and those of his family who survived were in the camp for seven months. The first three were the most terrifying, when the epidemics raged and death was omnipresent. During this period, some of the Jews became so desperate and frightened that they tried to return to Ethiopia. Most of them did not make it.

"How many old and young people had dreamed of returning to Zion—but by the will of God, they remained on the way!" He said that he felt saddest for the elderly who had made the long journey dreaming at least of a burial in the Holy Land. "It will take a long time, maybe a generation or more, before the terror, horror, and agony of Umm Rekuba will pass. I'm still in shock," he said, two months after his rescue.

At that time, Yosef still had not told his three-year-old son that Rachel, his mother, had died. The boy kept asking him when Rachel would "return from the clinic" and told his father to take her food every day. Yosef kept promising his son that "your mother will come home tomorrow."

"When the boy wakes at night and cries for his mother, the only thing I can do is to cry with him and his brothers. It's difficult to cope. I'm not sure what to do."

ALL THE PEOPLE in the village of Telempt, near Gondar, picked up and left one day in January 1984. Ya'acov, a forty-year-old farmer whose Ethiopian name is Sarala, told his twelve-year-old son, "We're going to Jerusalem."

Ya'acov had heard stories that "if we got to Sudan, we would be brought to the Holy Land." A group of Tigre Liberation Front guerrillas, Christians, had been holing up in the village. They told the Jewish villagers that government troops would not stop them from going to Sudan, and offered to lead them to the border for money.

"We sold our cows, most of our horses, sheep, grain, everything we owned, and gave about half the money to our guides. Two hundred and eighty people, the whole village, set out with 25 horses and 160 mules," Ya'acov said. They had ample provisions of flour and jerry cans of water, and they cooked unleavened bread—matzo, called *kita*—along the way.

After walking for seven days, they reached a place called Mahausay, in Tigre Province. Their guides told them that they would have to stay there for a while, because of fighting between the Tigrean insurgents and government forces. It was three months before they moved on.

After leaving Mahausay, they walked for ten days through rolling hills into mountainous country in the Wolkait region and camped there for a month. On the last leg of the journey, they walked through bleached desert for seven days to a point near the Sudan border, where they sold their mules and horses for the equivalent of about fifteen dollars each. Most of that money was paid in bribes to Sudanese border guards.

They crossed into Sudan at Zefa and walked another day and night through the desert, carrying their remaining jerry cans of water on their backs. Some

members of their group were split off by the Sudanese authorities and sent to another camp. The
main group reached Wad el-Heluw camp, where they
were immediately admitted. The party had not lost
one person along the way. But soon after they arrived in the camp in May, the villagers of Telempt
died in droves.

Ya'acov says it was "the new food" that was responsible for the deaths. But it was undoubtedly the
contaminated water and unsanitary, crowded conditions that led to the epidemics and the death of
about half of the people in his group. His own immediate family survived, although he did not know
the fate of his mother, who tried to go back to Ethiopia with one of his brothers.

LEAH, A DIGNIFIED woman in her seventies, was the
daughter of a famous Falasha holy man, a legendary
figure. As a baby, her father was saved from a croc-
odile by Leah's grandfather, who killed the animal
with a sword at a place on the northern shore of Lake
Tana. It was said that the rescued infant would have
an illustrious future. Indeed, he became an important religious leader of the Ethiopian Jews and
preached that the Falashas would return to Zion
within a few years.

How did Leah hear about the escape path to Israel? "The news came with the wind," she said,
holding her hands up and opening her eyes wide. "The
news of the redemption came with the wind."

Leah was told by friendly Christian neighbors that
the Jews were going to Israel but that the journey
wasn't worth it for old people like her. "Some of our
old people stayed because they did not think that they

could survive the trip. I knew I could make it," the gray-haired matriarch said.

She walked for two days to a nearby village to find out if it was true that the Ethiopian Jews were going to Israel. It soon became apparent to her that "this was the hour of redemption" (a phrase repeated over and over again by the Falashas who reached Israel).

"Old people went along with the young people, walking days and nights, not tired, not hungry, not thirsty, not sick—for we knew we were going to the Holy Land. Our belief was constantly strengthened. We were not afraid, and we walked by day and did not sneak out at night. Our group of six families, about one hundred people, paid two hundred birr (one hundred dollars) per family to a Christian to guide us. Just before we left, the Ethiopian government authorities called our villagers to a gathering and warned us that if we tried to leave the country, our men would be punished. A second such meeting was called and again they warned us against leaving. But it was impossible to stop us. The gentile officials argued with each other about what to do with us. They didn't know what to do. Finally, the officials gave in. They saw that if we were not allowed to leave, they would have no alternative but to imprison or kill us all.

"The danger of bandits, or of snakes, leopards, and other animals, did not deter us. We walked for six weeks, including every Shabbat, with little food."

When the Falashas arrived in the desert region, they hired a local man to guide them through the wilderness. They walked every morning from 3 A.M. until about 11 A.M., then sought shelter from the relentless sun until late afternoon, when they resumed walking for a few hours. Along the way, they met other groups of Falashas, and their original number swelled to over eighty. Three members of the original group died along the way.

They built rafts to cross the river along the border. But soon after they reached the other side, they were stopped and questioned by a Sudanese police patrol. The police took all of their money, beat them brutally, called for two trucks, and shipped them back across the border, abandoning them in the middle of the desert. "We were left there with nothing—no food, water, money. We were in shock and really thought that this was the end," Leah said. But they remained undeterred from their goal.

Just before crossing the river a second time, her group was attacked by bandits, who stripped them of their belongings. Leah, like many other Ethiopian Jews who told of their ordeal, was too ashamed to relate that the women in the group were raped.

"We were lucky to cross the river. But after that, fierce rains came, and we were trapped in the mud. What kept us alive and walking was the hope for freedom, for salvation. At one stage we walked in the sea of mud for three days."

A day later, they met a group of Sudanese who were sympathetic and led them to a Red Cross station a day's walk away. The Red Cross people took them to a refugee camp, but within hours, they were being interrogated again by Sudanese police. "They asked us if we were Jews. We denied it and hid our prayer books. We told them we had come in search of food, because of the famine. But they said that the situation in Ethiopia was improving and that they were going to send us back. They sent for a truck. We begged them on our knees, and this time, the police did not send us back to the desert.

"The Red Cross people couldn't believe that we had made it through such difficult territory. We were sent to Tuwawa, near Umm Rekuba. We were there for months. We witnessed great suffering there. We warned our children not to say that they were Jews, or they might be killed.

"Fear, murder, immorality, beatings, horror reigned in the camps. The Red Cross gave us oil and flour. We heard that many Jews were in Umm Rekuba and that many had already gotten to Israel. My husband's brother was sent to Umm Rekuba, where he died along with many other people. If the rest of us had been sent there, we would have died too. Umm Rekuba was the place of death."

5

Mother
of
Plague

The refugee
camp called Umm Rekuba (Mother of Shelter, in Arabic), lies about forty miles from the Ethiopian border, close to where the vast, stony wilderness of Sudan
is suddenly interrupted by the wind-worn foothills
that lead to the Ethiopian plateau. It is not inviting
country. A decade of drought has devastated the land,
and the Beja people of the region, half a million nomads, face extinction.

The camp had been established in the mid-1970s

for two thousand Ethiopian refugees, but by mid-1984, about twenty thousand were living in either *tukuls* or tents. The camp, with a few pan-roofed shops, a clinic, a school, and a church, was de facto divided into two, between Christian and Jewish Ethiopians.

Umm Rekuba was administered by the Sudan Commission for Refugees and the country's Council of Churches, in conjunction with the office of the United Nations High Commissioner for Refugees, which was entirely responsible for administering the distribution of food supplies. Two Swedish evangelical missionaries helped run the camp. It was the main habitation of Ethiopian Jewish refugees, who were also housed at Tuwawa and at smaller camps in the Gedaref area.

When the Falashas arrived there after trekking through Ethiopia for periods ranging from two weeks to over three months, they were exhausted, dehydrated, weak from hunger, terrified. The drastic change in climate from the highlands to the desert region had weakened them further. The facilities at Umm Rekuba were thoroughly inadequate, and two thousand Jews would die there.

The worst period began in June 1984, just after the last Mossad flight from the desert between Umm Rekuba and Tuwawa. Hundreds of Jews at Umm Rekuba and nearby Wad el-Heluw succumbed to disease brought on mostly by contaminated water from a nearby river. During the short rainy season that normally begins around July, the river rises rapidly. But with temperatures above 110 degrees during most of the year, the river soon dries up, and only a few pools of water are left. The rivers of the region dried up earlier than usual in recent years as the drought

worsened and the huge North African desert continued moving southward. The shallow puddles were
shared by camels, donkeys, wild animals, and refugees. Excreta and the bloated carcasses of dead animals floated in the muddy, septic pools.

This water, left untreated, was poured into old
barrels and distributed in the camp—one steel bar-
rel for every ten tents or mud huts. Within minutes,
the receptacles would be emptied, the water carried
away by refugees hugging bottles and makeshift con-
tainers. Those possessing such vessels were considered to be exceedingly fortunate. Some of the
Falasha women traded their delicately crafted ear-
rings of soft Ethiopian gold for a jug. Ironically, the
water they drank to survive in the stifling heat also
carried the seeds of death. In Tuwawa, water was
trucked in from Gedaref; it proved to be only slightly
less contaminated.

Umm Rekuba and Tuwawa were among the older
camps in the region. At new camps, such as Wad
Kawli to the south, the conditions were generally even
more overcrowded and wretched. Scores perished
every day in the makeshift hospitals, where hundreds
of infirm, exhausted refugees were spread out on straw
mats in the dirt. A handful of Western and African
medical volunteers tended small children whose heads
looked terribly big, helping them to hold plastic
glasses containing nourishment. All around the camps
swirled clouds of dust, rising from convoys of trucks
shuttling refugees between the various "sanctums."
At one camp near Tuwawa, Abu Raham (Father of
Mercy), the refugees chanted and played drums late
into the night, praying for the dying to recover. Some
of the camps appeared to be tent cities; others had a

more settled look, with walled compounds and round mud and grass huts.

The camp at Umm Rekuba experienced constant shortages of medicine, food, and blankets for the chilly desert nights. Elizabeth Broberg, one of the two Swedish nurses, arrived at the camp in May 1984 and later recalled her first impression: "People were lying all over the place. . . . There was a lot of sickness, everything you can imagine. The Falashas were afraid of medical care, didn't want anything to do with it. Some of them practiced bloodletting. Then came the measles, first in the reception center, but it spread throughout the camp. It was incredible how many died."

The food situation was even more difficult for the Jews than for the other refugees, since the Falashas would not eat certain things—unkosher cooking oil, for example. Their fear of violating the kosher laws, of becoming like the "abominable idolators"—Christian Ethiopians who eat raw meat—was stronger than their fear of starvation. One English health worker who visited the camp said that the Falashas were worse off than the other refugees because they often refused contact with the gentile medical workers and only accepted help when it was forced upon them. "They seemed sad, silent people, closed to the outside world," the worker said. "Unlike the Christians, they hardly communicated with us at all." One of the reasons for that mistrust was the attitude of some of the Christian refugees, who called the Falashas "killers of Jesus" and blamed them for the African famine and the pestilence.

Why didn't the Israelis send doctors to help the Ethiopian Jews? They did. The Mossad regularly dispatched medical teams composed of people of various nationalities to Umm Rekuba and the other camps where the Jews were concentrated, such as Maskar and Wad el-Heluw. But the doctors couldn't do much more than the nurses. Pediatricians could not deal with epidemiological problems; the Israelis could not rebuild the camps and throw out the Sudanese administration. Throughout the summer of 1984, when the worst epidemics raged, the Israeli medical personnel could offer little help.

"The problem was the camp itself and its administration—it was a sanitation nightmare," said one informed source. "The Israelis conducted a first-class operation, built up a tremendous infrastructure and used only the very best people. But what could a surgeon do when the water remained contaminated and there was not enough food? Or when the patient stopped drinking entirely? The people who died couldn't have been saved. The only way to save them was to get them out of the camps. The Israelis spent masses of money and there was total commitment. The goal of the mission was to bring people out. Nothing was done that could have jeopardized that aim. The Mossad was not in a position to dismantle the camp and disperse the refugees."

Relief workers and camp residents later told visitors that the camp went without food for three weeks in midsummer and that the death rate had been especially high in July and August, when the brief rainy season turned the roads into nearly impassable rivers of mud. "They had dysentery, malaria, dehydration, cholera, typhoid—everything," according to a nurse from the Sudan Council of Churches.

It appears that the UNHCR was responsible through

Ambover, the largest Falasha village, in 1976

Young Ambover woman weaving a basket

Unless otherwise credited, all photos by Louis Rapoport

Falasha potters in front of a *tukul* (hut)

Young shepherd tending a small herd of cattle outside Ambover

A *kes* (priest) with a Torah in the liturgical language Ge'ez

Young Falasha women studying to become teachers: Gondar, 1976

THIS PAGE: Gondar, the former capital of Ethiopia—in the heart of Falasha country

FACING PAGE: Yona Bogala, who helped pave the way to Israel for many Ethiopian Jews

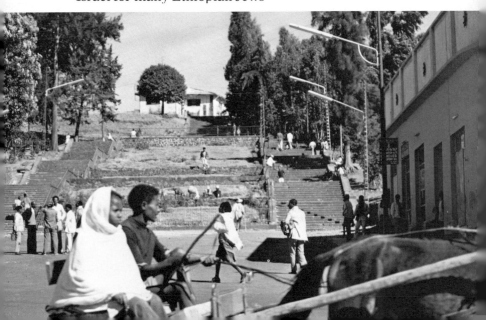

Falashas newly arrived at the Ashkelon transit center in Israel, December 1984

Jewish Agency workers, including a veteran Ethiopian immigrant, with new Falasha arrivals at the Acre transit center, March 1985

Falasha children about to leave Acre for Israeli absorption center, March 1985

A reunited family at Acre, March 1985

Hebrew teacher with her Ethiopian students in Safad,
April 1985

Prime Minister Shimon Peres with Falasha religious
leaders in Jerusalem, September 1985

Photo by Dan La

its negligence for the food shortages, and for ignoring the reports of large-scale deaths in the camps. In fact, the organization did not admit to its stockpiling and local procurement problems in eastern Sudan until November 1984, when it finally issued emergency appeals for aid. This was months after the epidemics and food shortages that killed thousands of refugees. Strangely, there was no outcry over the UN agency's negligence; it never made the headlines.

The UNHCR had been queried about the situation by the U.S. government as early as June 1984. The senior of the two nurses at Umm Rekuba, Anders Maltson, had gone to Khartoum to report to the UN office there and to the refugee affairs coordinator at the U.S. embassy, Jerry Weaver. Weaver, who would soon help to organize the mechanics of the Operation Moses airlift, visited the camp and cabled Washington about the desperate condition of the Jewish refugees. "The situation was really appalling," he recalled later. Hundreds had already died—as many as five hundred. "We visited the clinic, the one the Swedes worked out of, and they didn't have any medicine. The supplementary feeding program was without food. Walking through, it was obvious that there were a lot of people just not eating. You could see it. Also, it was raining around then, so the sanitation situation was just horrendous, because the Falashas would not go out of their grass huts. They were urinating and defecating in their *tukuls*, and some of these huts contained as many as ten, twelve, fifteen people."

State Department refugee official Richard Krieger, a political appointee who came from a background of Jewish community service, was outraged when he read Weaver's cables and sought immediate answers from UNHCR headquarters in Geneva. Krieger, who would prove to be one of the two pivotal American officials involved in the initiating of Operation Moses, got unsatisfactory answers from generally evasive UNHCR officials.

The UN agency sent an "investigator" who reported back that there were no shortages of food and medicine and that the death rate was "normal." In Khartoum, Weaver soon determined that the investigator never even visited Umm Rekuba, and the UNHCR later admitted that its man had only relied on "informed sources." After that, Weaver made sure that U.S.-supplied food got out to the camp, but it was still not enough, and the water supply was not improved. The death toll kept rising. The refugees were terribly weakened by a diet far below the UNHCR's minimum daily sustenance level of one pound of flour and one tablespoon each of dried milk, edible oil, and peas. A Jewish medical worker from North America who spent most of 1984 in the camps told me in September of that year that "thousands of refugees, including hundreds of Jews, died because the UNHCR only provided half of this meager sustenance. The refugees got an average of only half a pound of day of all the foods together."

The AAEJ was publicizing the fact that an average of about fifteen Jews were dying every day in the camps. And Simcha Jacobovici, a publicist living in Canada, wrote in the *New York Times* that thirteen hundred Falashas had died in the camps. But questions arose about Jacobovici's credibility because of the fantastic conspiracy charges he made in the article against some Israeli officials, who in fact had nothing to do with rescue policy.

The UNHCR kept denying that the deaths were occurring. On September 18, 1984, Philip Sargisson, an official at UNHCR headquarters in Geneva, told me that "reports that there are hundreds of dead refugees are inaccurate. Only a total of 150 have died over the past few months." He said that the deputy chief of his unit had left the previous day to "check out the reports." But the UNHCR never admitted the real facts of the situation, even though sources within the UNHCR told the Paris newspaper *Figaro* that the stories of wholesale death were true. Nor was there any inquiry into the circumstances in which several thousand people died.

The death toll and general situation at Umm Rekuba were described in several press reports beginning in September, including articles in the *Toronto Globe and Mail*, the *Jerusalem Post*, and the Paris journal *Libération*, as well as in *Figaro*. But still no UNHCR relief was sent to the Umm Rekuba camp— no doctor, not enough medicine, and no improvement in the water supply, although more food was made available, thanks to the Americans.

The North American nurse told me that the UNHCR chief in Sudan, Nicholas Morris of Australia, was aware that food had not reached the camps in the critical summer months and that he and his agency had covered up the extent of the deaths. One chronicler of these events has defended Morris, quoting a friend of the UNHCR chief as saying that when Morris went on leave in June 1984 "he seemed to be unaware of the crisis." Blame was placed on Peter Parr, director of the Gedaref suboffice of the UNHCR, who was later replaced. But even as late as January 1985, when I spoke to a harried Nicholas Morris in Khartoum, he maintained the denials of any severe food shortages during the previous summer: "We had enough food then," he said through gritted teeth.

The inadequacies of the UNHCR should have been of international concern, since the agency plays a key role in refugee relief worldwide, with the United States supplying most of the raw materials for the program. As reports of the UNHCR's problems emerged, the UN secretariat set up an Office for Emergency Operations in Africa to coordinate the efforts of the various governments, organizations, and private agencies helping the twenty countries affected by the famine. It was an indirect slap at the UNHCR.

The North American nurse, who returned home by way of Jerusalem in September 1984, also talked to Israeli government officials and Mossad people about what he saw in the camps. (The Mossad was well aware of the situation, getting regular reports from its medical teams in eastern Sudan.) "I now understand for the first time why the people who escaped from concentration camps but who couldn't get anyone to believe what was happening committed suicide," the nurse told me at the time. "A major disaster is happening to all the refugees . . . but the Falashas are the most vulnerable, and they're dying in greater numbers.

"The first time I came upon the Ethiopian Jews, I saw about sixty of them being unloaded from a Sudanese army truck. They sat quietly under a straw canopy huddled together in concentric circles—a few elderly people, women in their twenties and thirties, and mostly young children. They were scared and passive with pleading eyes. A minor camp official who was standing beside me observing the scene—a man

I rather liked—said suddenly, 'Falashas—look at them, not even people, they look like animals, behave like animals, dirty, uneducated, primitive. They have no knowledge of civilization.' And of course, the other refugees despised them even more—for they also feared that the Falashas were sorcerers, possessors of the evil eye.

"The Jewish refugees were dehydrated, sick, weak, wearing only the remnants of their clothes, some with embroidered Stars of David. Most of them were under the impression that it was only a matter of days before their final redemption. But it would be a long, cruel wait. Within weeks, even those who had arrived in good health were malnourished and sick. The camp manager, who was both very charming and extremely corrupt, distributed supplies according to his whim. Some refugees received food once a month, some almost not at all. Even when there were no shortages, not all of the food was distributed. It was no wonder that people started to die of starvation."

The medical worker, who had been a refugee in Europe as a child, continued: "In the refugee experience, confusion and insecurity envelop one's mind. There's the haunting fear about loved ones left behind or guilt about loved ones who died before your very eyes." The Beta-Israel refugees appeared to him to be more confused and in worse condition than the other refugees, afraid of the Christian Ethiopians and apprehensive of the Sudanese. "They were gripped by fear, huddled together in one area of the camp. On one occasion, I found twenty-seven people occupying one grass hut, fifteen feet in diameter. They hunched over a four-gallon plastic jerry can. If one of them took sick, the whole group was threatened. Often, an en-

tire family would succumb when some disease ravaged a single hut. There wasn't any barbed wire at
the camp, no guards kicking people—yet the images
of concentration camps were constantly in my mind's
eye. Here in front of me was another Jewish community being extinguished."

Although many of the Ethiopian Jews later reported a breakdown in morality in the camps, the
medical worker said that in general, the Beta-Israel
had maintained their dignity. While the rest of the
camp was rife with venereal disease, not one case of
VD occurred among the Falashas who came to the
clinic. In the therapeutic feeding program—a last-
resort effort to save the extremely malnourished—a
parent or sibling would have to spend a whole day
feeding a child through a naso-gastric tube. This is a
slow, painful, and mostly futile process, and few refugees had the stamina to participate. Many parents,
having to care for their other children, felt they had
no choice but to abandon the most malnourished in
the feeding station. "Yet the Beta-Israel would be
there day after day, never abandoning their sick. The
community, even in the most dire of situations, managed to organize itself and to help as much as possible."

Several Falashas chose to return to Ethiopia rather
than stay in the lethal environment of the camps.
When they reached their villages, they warned their
people that if they managed to survive the trek, they
wouldn't survive the camps. But this did not dis-
courage hundreds more from heading toward Sudan.
Many of them were apprehended by Ethiopian troops
and imprisoned. Their interrogators consistently demanded to know who had influenced them, who had

incited them to leave Ethiopia for Israel. The almost
uniform reply was, "It is foretold in the Bible: this is
the hour of our redemption."

One large group of the Beta-Israel caught by the
army near the Sudan border told the soldiers that they
were en route to "Jerusalem-Zion." They were taken
to a military base, where an interrogating officer was
told the same thing over and over again: "Jerusalem-Zion." He thought that they were insane and ordered their immediate release. Another group of 150,
led by a Falasha priest carrying a Torah, were stopped
near Sudan and trucked back to the central prison in
Gondar, where they were imprisoned for four months.
They all signed the guarantee that they wouldn't try
to escape again, on penalty of death. But all of them
made it to Umm Rekuba in October 1984, just before
the big rescue operation. By that time there were almost two thousand cairns in the Falasha burial
grounds next to the camp. No one had the strength
to dig graves.

IN JUNE 1984, when Israeli agents radioed Jerusalem
from Sudan about the rising death toll in the camps,
the Mossad and Israeli government officials were
stymied about what to do. No special "secret cabinet
meetings about the Falashas" were called by Prime
Minister Yitzhak Shamir, as one report would have
it, but the subject was brought up periodically at the
regular Sunday cabinet sessions. The cabinet, however, was not involved in any decision making. This
was left in the hands of the prime minister and the
Mossad's operations chief, Joshua, an old friend of
Shamir's from his years in the Mossad. Nor did the
Foreign Ministry have any major role to play: the

Mossad reports directly to the Prime Minister's Office.

The Ethiopian Jews were not Israel's only interest in Sudan, and the score of agents who were based in Sudan had many other tasks to perform besides the rescue operations. Sudan—strategically located between Egypt and radical Libya to the north and Soviet-backed Ethiopia to the southeast, and just across the narrow Red Sea from Saudi Arabia—has long been considered to be of major importance to the Israeli intelligence community. A spy master's dream, it was a listening post and a crossroads where vital information concerning the Horn of Africa and the Middle East was gathered by various intelligence services.

Israelis had been in the Sudan many years before the influx of Ethiopian refugees began. They trained insurgent Christian and animist black tribes in the south in an attempt to weaken Arab domination over Africa's largest country. After President Nimeiry reached an agreement with the rebels, the Israeli agents in Sudan focused on other aspects of the spy business. Their work was considered indispensable by old hands like Joshua and by the prime minister, who had once tracked Nazi scientists in Nasser's Egypt and been chief of Israeli intelligence operations in Europe.

It is fair to surmise that one of the reasons Shamir and the Mossad turned to the Americans for help at this crucial moment was that they hoped to preserve the carefully built-up Israeli intelligence structure in Sudan, which included a secret base of operations, sophisticated communications systems, even a thriving business operation. But it soon became obvious that any major action to save the Falashas, whether sponsored by the Americans or not, would probably put an end to the Israeli intelligence operations. In the end, Shamir put the lives of the Ethiopian Jews in the refugee camps ahead of important Israeli security interests.

Ambassador Meir Rosenne at the Israeli embassy in Washington was instructed to appeal to the White House to intervene with Sudan's president and to help the Mossad arrange an airlift of the seven to ten thousand Falashas still in the camps. It was a request that was fraught with problems for the U.S. administration, which did not want to see its excellent relations with Sudan damaged. On the other hand, it was a major humanitarian question, and several American officials and legislators had been campaigning for some time for a rescue involving the United States.

Shamir met with leaders of the Beta-Israel community in Israel and told them, "We are doing the maximum despite the obstacles and difficulties." Shamir said that money was no problem, that great efforts were under way "because there is no price too great for saving lives."

Shimon Peres formed a new government in late summer 1984, and when he became prime minister in September, he too took a personal interest in the immigration of the Ethiopian Jews. But Shamir, who became vice prime minister and foreign minister in the national unity coalition government, was kept in charge of the Falasha *aliyah*.

Within the Mossad, a sharp difference of opinion emerged between the twenty agents in the field in Sudan and Joshua in Jerusalem. The agents pressed

for a massive Israeli airlift in the briefest period possible—several planes every night for a week in the
desert outside Gedaref. This was exactly what the
Americans were afraid of, an event which might create an international incident that could destabilize the
Nimeiry government or cause a rupture between the
United States and Sudan. But Joshua vetoed the En-
tebbe-type plan suggested by his agents, saying that
it was simply too risky and that if it were interrupted for any reason, it might also derail American
efforts to rescue the Falashas "quietly."

According to State Department officials, the initiative for Operation Moses did not come from the Israelis, but from the department itself. Israeli sources
adamantly deny this. They insist that the Mossad took
the lead, adding that the government in Jerusalem is
constrained from discussing this for security reasons. Yitzhak Shamir told me several months after
Operation Moses that lives were still at stake.

The chief refugee official at the U.S. embassy in
Khartoum, Jerry Weaver, gave *Los Angeles Times*
correspondent Charles Powers an interview that
formed the basis for a ten-thousand-word story the
paper ran in early July 1985. That story assigned the
credit for Operation Moses to Jerry Weaver. Weaver
is a former UCLA professor who was known as an
undiplomatic "cowboy" in Khartoum and was
thought by many to be the CIA chief in the country—
probably an erroneous assumption. But he also had
a reputation for getting things done. In fact, Weaver
did perform brilliantly in orchestrating the rescue
operations. But he was not the "mastermind" of the
action, as the newspaper called him, and he was not
alone. It was Washington's clout in Sudan that made

Operation Moses possible, and no single official could claim all the credit.

Two U.S. State Department officials, Deputy Assistant Secretary for East Africa Princeton Lyman and Richard Krieger, were instrumental in getting the United States to back a plan to cooperate with Israel in a rescue. "They were the driving force," according to another State Department official closely involved with the rescue of the Ethiopian Jews. "The Israelis didn't come to us until August, months after things got rolling on this end." Other U.S. government sources have said that the Israelis never approached the Americans, that it was strictly a U.S. initiative. "The Israelis agreed to it in the first week of July. We came to them."

But what these State Department officials didn't know was that Israel and the United States had been discussing the problem on a different level since the spring, in talks between the Mossad and the Prime Minister's Office on the one hand and the CIA and the White House on the other.

The Reagan administration, acting on Mossad and CIA reports, informed the Nimeiry government of its concern for the Ethiopian Jews in the camps. Nimeiry was reportedly not happy about the U.S. interest but told his No. 2 man, First Vice President and Chief of the Secret Police Omar Tayeb, to keep tabs on the situation. Nimeiry was in desperate need for an increase in aid from the United States, and he sensed an emerging opportunity.

In early June 1984, Richard Krieger had a discussion with a top Sudanese official, whom Nimeiry had sent to Washington to appeal for more aid: food for his country, refugee relief, as well as military support because of the renewed insurgency in southern Sudan. Krieger, aware of the high death rate in the camps from the reports by Weaver, the AAEJ, and others, saw a chance to get all of the Falashas out. He put the Sudanese official on hold.

The next day, Krieger convened a meeting of a small group of American officials in the office of the U.S. Coordinator of Refugees in the State Department and brought up proposals for a U.S. role in airlifting the Ethiopian Jews. In subsequent meetings that week, Krieger and his superior, Ambassador H. Eugene Douglas, head of the refugee division, told the key Sudanese official that if more aid for Sudan were to be allocated, it would be crucial to get support from the American Jewish lobby. The way to do that, they said, was for the Sudanese to help America take the Ethiopian Jews out of the refugee camps. Nimeiry's emissary was given to understand that the Americans would probably increase aid to Sudan by $50 million to a total of $250 million for 1985. The "deal" was made then and there, but it would take four months to close it.

(Later there was a great deal of speculation that millions of dollars in cash had greased the palms of Sudanese officials. Rumors abounded that huge sums had been made available by a Sudanese-born Jewish tycoon, Nessim Gaon, who lives in Geneva; or that Saudi billionaire Adnan Khashoggi—known to be a close friend of Nimeiry's—had acted as an intermediary; or that the paymaster had been an American Jewish lawyer with interests in Sudan. But there is nothing to substantiate these stories. The Mossad did spend perhaps $3 million in the Sudan over a four-year period, and some people did receive *baksheesh* in the early actions before the airlift. But the only cash involved in Operation Moses itself was $1 million that the Israelis would give to Jerry Weaver to spend on transport, supplies, and communications systems.)

The head of the State Department's African bureau, Chester Crocker, and Princeton Lyman, who had become aware of the Falashas' plight during a tour of duty in the 1970s at the embassy in Addis Ababa, joined with Krieger in formulating the rescue plan. They sought and obtained the agreement of Ambassador Hume Horan in Khartoum. "Lyman's knowledge of the workings of the department—he handled the red tape—and the willingness of men like Crocker and Horan to risk their careers by pushing Krieger's plan is what made it all happen," according to one informed source. "It was a proposition the Israelis couldn't refuse." Memorandum writing—the habitual occupation of State Department employees—was kept to a minimum for fear that the plan would be revealed to "Arabist" elements within the department.

Arrangements for Operation Moses were made at a relatively low State Department level, although the officials concerned did obtain the acquiescence of Deputy Under Secretary of State Richard Murphy, who was in overall charge of Middle East diplomacy. A formal department memorandum on the plan went up the ladder to Secretary of State George Shultz at the end of June.

Some concern was expressed in the department that too much was being done for so few refugees. Officials were worried that U.S. relations with Sudan and the Arab world would be endangered if the story broke. Because of the reluctance, "a lot of chits were burned to get the plan through," according to one source. But an irresistible moral force was involved. Forty years earlier, several State Department officials, led by Breckinridge Long, barred Jewish refugees from entering the United States and blocked efforts directed at rescuing Jews in Romania and Hungary, actions that contributed to the deaths of hundreds of thousands. In the modern State Department, a number of officials felt that it was incumbent on the United States to do everything possible to help Jewish refugees anywhere. "A fortunate convergence of opinion about the Ethiopian Jews prevailed among this small group of Jewish and gentile officials in the department. If Gene Douglas had said no, there wouldn't have been a program. Any one of the middle-ranking guys could have stopped it, but they put the importance of saving lives ahead of their careers," the source said.

Liaison with the Israelis was placed in the hands of Lyman and Krieger. On July 5, 1984, Krieger flew to Israel to organize the airlift with the Israelis, who one American official felt had been doing "a magnificent job but on a limited basis." Krieger then went on to Geneva to finalize the agreement with the Sudanese. At that point, all the parties involved were agreed in principle, but communications and logistics remained to be worked out.

The Israelis at first demanded to meet Sudanese officials head to head, but the State Department had to say no. "It was never out of our hands," according to one department source. "It would curl your hair to know what went on with the Israelis. They are such a pain in the ass to deal with." He added that the most difficult Israelis were Foreign Ministry personnel. In contrast, the Israeli Mossad people were efficient and straightforward, especially Joshua, the chief Mossad organizer. "Some great people—Israeli heroes—were involved, but their names will never be known," another American official remarked. Of the "public" Israelis he mentioned, Yehuda Dominitz of the Jewish Agency and Moshe Gilboa of the Foreign Ministry were said to have been most helpful.

In August, consultations continued in Washington involving Lyman, Douglas, and Krieger; Elliott Abrams, assistant secretary for human rights; and department refugee officials James Purcell, Jr., and Arthur E. Dewey. Several of these officials flew to Geneva later in the month to confer separately with Israeli and Sudanese officials.

Public concern was mounting in the United States for the fate of the Ethiopian Jews, and congressional debate on the subject was held in September, at the same time that the secret efforts proceeded. Yitzhak Shamir flew to Washington for talks with Secretary Shultz, during which they discussed the evolving plan to airlift the Falashas out of Sudan.

A key meeting was held early that month in Geneva, at which Lyman, Krieger, the U.S. mission chief in Geneva, Joshua, Yehuda Dominitz, Jerry Weaver, and some officials of an international organization took part. It was at this meeting and a subsequent one on Rosh Hashanah, the Jewish New Year, that the technical details were worked out. "Weaver was just one of our people. He was never involved until this September meeting, long after the operation had been initiated by the State Department. He wasn't even at the August Geneva meetings," said one of the participants in all of the sessions. But Weaver's reports, along with updates provided by Israeli intelligence, underlined the urgent need for action.

Weaver was instructed to use his contacts with the Sudanese secret service to set up a meeting with its chief, Omar el-Tayeb.

In their talks in Khartoum, Ambassador Horan and Weaver told Tayeb that the Falashas, who were dying at a much higher rate than the other refugees, were becoming an international problem, and for various reasons it was in the interests of Sudan and the United States to solve the quandary by airlifting the Ethiopian Jews out of Africa. Tayeb, who probably was unaware of the Mossad's efforts over the last four years to bring out thousands of Falashas, agreed to go along with the Americans. Weaver was designated as the contact man, and two colonels connected to the security service were to work with him. President Nimeiry himself was not directly involved.

Weaver also operated with some of the score of Mossad agents in Sudan. All of the paperwork for Operation Moses was done by Mossad operatives in cooperation with American embassy personnel and representatives of international refugee organizations.

Weaver, together with the Mossad and the Sudanese secret police, came up with the operation plan in October 1984. The refugees would follow one of the Mossad's old routes. They would be driven to a meeting place just outside Tuwawa and from there directly to the Khartoum airport, five hours away. Chartered aircraft, not military planes, would then fly them to Europe and thence to Israel. One Israeli official who was at the Geneva meetings later told a reporter that he thought Weaver was a loser at first, "but by the second day I was a believer. We were talking about having some agency do some task or other, and Weaver was saying, 'No, if you do this, you're going to have an unholy mess on your hands,' and he explained why. And the more I listened, the more I realized he knew what he was doing."

Upon his return to Sudan, Weaver set about buying four buses and five other long-range vehicles, black-market fuel, food, blankets, and communications gear, and arranging for safe houses in Gedaref and Khartoum.

The Mossad arranged for the planes. Belgium's Trans European Airways (TEA) had been flying Sudanese pilgrims to Mecca for years and thus aroused no suspicion by its presence at Khartoum's tiny international airport. TEA's owner, Georges Gutelman, an Orthodox Jew, reportedly had close ties with the Mossad. The Israelis promised him ample compensation for the inevitable loss of the Mecca route once the story broke. And, according to one report, Gutelman felt that by switching routes from Mecca to Jerusalem, "he would be able to play a role in the redemption of the Jewish people." Gutelman enlisted the support of the Belgian government through his friend and coreligionist Jean Gol, then vice premier and justice minister. Hundreds of TEA workers would become involved in the operation, without any leaks to the media. TEA air crews stayed at the Friendship Palace Hotel on the outskirts of Khartoum, where many journalists from around the world were based while covering the big African drought and refugee stories. "I never would have guessed what they were up to," a *Newsweek* correspondent said later.

A month before the airlift was to begin, the alert

went out to about one thousand Israelis, who were told to get ready for the massive influx. Yehuda and his wife, Rina, helped organize the social workers, translators, medical personnel, and women soldiers who would receive the Ethiopian Jews. The Mossad also asked Yehuda to pick a veteran Israeli Falasha to go to the Sudan immediately. He chose "Aleph," an old friend and distant relative, a quiet-spoken college graduate. Aleph was to work primarily with Jerry Weaver, identifying the Falashas in the camp and getting them ready for the flights.

The airlift was set for November 1, then postponed to November 10, and finally to November 20. The postponements were caused by local considerations, such as coordination with the Sudanese secret police and the condition of the roads. But the delays set off rumors among some of the Israeli Falashas who were involved that some enemy of the Beta-Israel in the Jewish Agency or in the cabinet had sabotaged the operation. This suspicion was groundless.

In Khartoum the Americans, the Sudanese secret police, the Belgian flight crews, and the Israeli agents and their helpers in various locations were all standing ready. Aleph flew to Khartoum via Europe on November 18 and was taken immediately to Gedaref by Weaver and his Sudanese assistant. On the morning of the nineteenth, a few hours after his arrival in Sudan, Aleph, still in a jet-lag haze, was taken to Tuwawa. "He had never been there, no one knew him," Weaver said of Aleph. "So he had to go in and introduce himself—'I am the son of . . . and I am here to take you out.' About two o'clock he comes out and he says, 'I think I've made contact, and I think we'll have the people tonight.' "

One of the Falasha elders at Tuwawa who welcomed Aleph said later, "We knew our brothers had come from Israel to help us. We knew our dream was being realized, and we were not afraid."

6

Out
of
Africa

Operation
Moses was about to get under way, and the Mossad
agents in Sudan were instructed to keep just out of
range, leaving many of the details to the Americans
and the Sudanese state security. The Mossad had
thrown Aleph into battle, and with little preparation
for what he was about to face. But the Israeli agents
were in every place that counted, including inside
the camps themselves. In Tuwawa, several agents
watched at a distance as Aleph walked into the camp.
His task was to make contact with the Falasha lead-

ership in the camps and then to help organize an orderly exodus.

The camp leadership that began to take shape in 1980 when Yehuda was in Sudan had degenerated seriously. There were, to be sure, genuinely altruistic leaders, such as "Z," a Falasha who spoke fluent English and served as the intermediary between the refugees and the people who ran Wad el-Heluw. (Z would become Aleph's key assistant in the camp.) But a few of the other leaders had enriched themselves by taking bribes from their fellow Jews who sought to be high up on the list of those getting out on the first flights. The Israeli-American plan was to take the sick, orphans, and the aged first, but some of these got pushed aside.

Several of the "list makers" went further in their avarice. Since 1980 Mossad agents had been bringing them large sums of cash to distribu e among the people. But, as it emerged later, only a ⟩ rtion of that money filtered down to the majority ot ⸤he refugees. In July and August 1984, when food was in short supply in Umm Rekuba and hundreds of people died, the list makers withheld tens of thousands of dollars from their fellow refugees, money that could have been used to buy local produce in Gedaref.

Why didn't the Mossad agents do something about these elements? Perhaps it was feared that if the Israelis took any forceful action, it would upset the ongoing operations. Perhaps there was the threat of blackmail; the list makers could easily have revealed the clandestine operation and stopped it cold. In any case, it wasn't surprising that the list makers plotted to kill Aleph the minute they set eyes on him: they sensed that he spelled the end of their operation.

Jerry Weaver's impression of Aleph was that he was

"timid and fragile," probably because of his slight build and soft-spoken Ethiopian manner. But Aleph was every bit as tough as Weaver. He was no stranger to war, having commanded men in the fight for the Golan Heights in 1973. In Sudan he would perform admirably, helping to calm down the hysterical, traumatized refugees and defying the list makers and their threats.

Aleph, a handsome thirty-five-year-old man whose brown face is dominated by the large round eyes that set Ethiopians apart from other Africans, had once been a leading activist for his community in Israel, lobbying and demonstrating to get the government to recognize the Falashas as Jews and to rescue them. In 1979 he had told a group of wealthy American Jews that seven thousand Falasha refugees were turning to the Jewish world for help, that they faced disaster. But the years of struggle and ugly internecine fighting between Tigre and Gondar Jews had embittered him. He had "dropped out" just before the great migration began at the beginning of the 1980s, turning all his energies to his family and to obtaining a master's degree at Hebrew University. Now, he was thrust back into action, to play a critical role in saving the Ethiopian Jews.

In an interview in 1974, in the early days of the Falashas' struggle, Aleph had told me that if an *aliyah* operation were ever to be mounted, there would be no difficulty identifying the Jews among the other Ethiopians even though they have the same physical characteristics. "We all know each other; we are linked by family." Ten years later, in the midst of the teeming refugees, it proved to be not so easy a task. But in the end, only a small number of non-Jews were included in the lists. Some of these people had been befriended by Falashas who later vouched for them as Jews. Some intermarriage had occurred, especially among the town dwellers. A few were children of slaves. (The Beta-Israel, like most Ethiopian peoples, had owned slaves.) Other non-Jews had bribed the list makers. Out of a total of about 15,000 Ethiopian refugees who were brought to Israel over a four-year period, about 120 were non-Jews.

As soon as Aleph entered Tuwawa and contacted his people, he realized what he was up against. A crowd of people surrounded him, at first groveling as they told him of the devastating epidemics of the summer, the continuing decimation of the Jewish refugees, and the urgency of their needs. But they soon started to turn mean and threatening. Arguments broke out while Aleph, flanked by the list makers, assured the growing crowd that they would all be in Israel in a few hours or in a few days. "Give me a chance to put things in order," he pleaded. He told them to disperse, that the whole operation would be canceled if the Christian population in the camp became aware of what was happening.

As the sun began to set, Aleph sent a steady stream of people out to the fields where Weaver and his Sudanese assistants were waiting for them. As they walked, the Falashas began shouting and shoving their way forward toward the waiting buses. Aleph emerged from the camp and pushed his way to the lead vehicle, standing in front of the closed door. Suddenly those in the crowd roared, flung Aleph aside, and tore at one another's clothes while clawing their way to the bus. Some of them tried to pry open the bars on the windows; others climbed on the roof of the bus.

Weaver grabbed a wooden staff from an old man and starting cracking people over the shoulders until they were driven back.

"By now it is six o'clock and dark. The Sudanese are nervous, I'm nervous, and obviously, the people getting on the buses are very nervous," Weaver would tell the *Los Angeles Times*. "By about 6:30, we have packed no one knows how many people aboard the buses, and we try to leave. People are running after us. Total pandemonium. In the confusion, we take the wrong road. We are driving on a dirt track parallel to the Gedaref-Khartoum highway, but we can't seem to get to it. So we stop the caravan, turn the whole damn thing around, and go back toward the camp and get on the highway.

"Now this is our maiden voyage. We've got a five-hour drive ahead of us. We had driven about fifteen or twenty minutes, and we come up to two policemen. They flash their light, and the convoy commander stops. The two cops come up and start asking who are you and what're these buses and who're these people. . . . ?"

Through bluff and persistence, they managed to get through the various checkpoints. In general, the Sudanese soldiers and police showed an inordinate amount of respect toward whites. Complete silence reigned on all four buses, which were crammed with people. When they arrived around midnight at a checkpoint some ten miles from the Khartoum airport, Sudanese secret police met them and said that the plane hadn't come in yet. It finally landed at 1:20 A.M. They entered the airport area through a back gate and boarded the Belgian charter plane on the night-parking apron, far away from the small, one-story passenger terminal.

The Boeing 707 was soon packed with 283 Ethiopian Jews. The Belgian pilot didn't want to take off with so many passengers. (The plane normally carries a maximum of 220.) But after an angry exchange with Weaver, the pilot relented. Operation Moses got off to a bumpy start as the first flight cleared the runway at 2:40 A.M., November 21, 1984.

The Mossad code name for the airlift operations was Gur Aryeh Yehuda, "The Lion of Judah's Cub," but this name was known by only a select few. "Operation Moses" was coined when the United Jewish Appeal launched a special fund-raising campaign in the United States at the time the airlift began. (The term has since been used also to describe the earlier efforts in which Ethiopian Jews were brought to Israel between 1980 and 1984 by plane and ship.)

The route for the first flight and all subsequent ones during the next six weeks was the same: Khartoum to Brussels—where the planes refueled—and then on to Tel Aviv. The empty Trans European Airways charter planes flew back to Khartoum via Athens.

While the main airlift was going on, small groups of Ethiopian Jews continued to be brought out via the original Mossad route, which had operated for four years. On the first day of Operation Moses, Yehuda accompanied forty-three other Ethiopian Jews on a flight from Khartoum to Athens and then on to Israel. Another thirty-six came four days later.

Before the fifth flight of the big airlift, Aleph told Weaver and his assistant that the list makers were creating great difficulties by continuing to exploit their dependents. Weaver decided it was time to take action. When the buses were loaded, he told the chief list maker to go into the first bus to count the passengers. Then he slammed the door and shouted orders to the Sudanese secret service officer inside: "Tell him to sit down, and if the son of a bitch moves, shoot him." After that, new list makers were chosen to assist Aleph.

After the rough start to the airlift, the kinks in the operation were gradually smoothed out, with the Sudanese state security agents keeping closer tabs. They accompanied the buses all along the route from the rendezvous to the airport, to avoid any delays at the checkpoints. Mossad people continued to keep watch over every aspect of the operation.

About sixty-four hundred people were brought out on twenty-eight flights from November 21 to January 5. At first, there was one flight from Sudan every forty-eight hours, the Sabbath excepted. In late December, the rate was increased to every twenty-four hours.

When the Ethiopian Jews landed at the military section of Ben-Gurion Airport, they were greeted first by Yehuda or another of the veteran Israeli Ethiopians. Ambulances carried about one out of every five passengers to Tel Hashomer Hospital in Tel Aviv, where doctors treated them for dehydration, typhoid, dysentery, and various tropical nightmares, such as onchocerciasis—river blindness. The others were whisked to transit centers, where their burlap rags were burned and they were given gym suits, tennis shoes, and air force parkas. Women soldiers joined government and Jewish Agency workers in helping the new immigrants, talking in sign language, using a few words of Amharic, and showing warmth and tenderness.

"I had never seen an airplane," said Dawit, who came from a village in the remote Semien Mountains, "and I thought it was a miracle from the heavens." He could not describe his happiness, except to say that he had the same wonderful feeling when a gracious Israeli woman presented him with the strange new clothes people wear in the Promised Land.

IN THE SAME week that the airlift was launched, the seeds for its miscarriage were being planted. Some Jewish leaders—and pro-Falasha activists as well— had not learned from the tragic consequences that result from loose talk or from gaffes such as Moshe Dayan's 1978 "slip of the tongue," which had halted a previous *aliyah*.

The secret operation began unraveling with the Israeli government's decision that the Jewish Agency should immediately seek funds for the operation from Jews abroad. On the day the airlift started, a high-ranking Israeli official met in secret with the top leaders of the United Jewish Appeal, American Jewry's main funding organization, at the Israeli consulate in Manhattan and requested them to gear up for a $60 million emergency campaign, one that had to be conducted as quietly as possible. The money would go to the Jewish Agency in Jerusalem.

Later, serious questions would be raised about the timing of the fund-raising, which by its very nature made news leaks more likely, and with them the likelihood that a politically embarrassed Sudan would halt the operation. The UJA–Jewish Agency campaign involved speeches, public meetings, and broad distribution of information that inevitably reached the press. The question of why this fund-raising had to be undertaken just as the operation got under way has never been answered satisfactorily. In the end, news leaks cost a number of lives and could have resulted in many more deaths. The agency's indiscretions were compounded by the Israeli government's errors. But the story of the leaks would be but a footnote to Operation Moses if it didn't reveal how things really work—or don't work—when a community confronts a life-and-death situation.

The leaders of the militant American and Canadian associations for Ethiopian Jews had been informed by American officials that the airlift was about to be launched and that silence was vital, but some of their more overzealous members continued to agitate, with newspaper advertisements, op-ed articles, and a demonstration that would indirectly set off the first news leaks about Operation Moses.

Major American and European newspapers, magazines, and broadcast media—along with most of the Jewish and Israeli press—cooperated with Israeli officials for several weeks in the autumn and winter of 1984 in embargoing publication of the story of the airlift rescue. Israel has the second biggest foreign press corps in the world, but none of the over three hundred members of the Foreign Press Association broke the story. But according to a *New York Times* correspondent, who was among the many journalists asked to keep the story out of the papers, "Jewish Agency officials in late November were boasting about the operation and patting themselves on the back at cocktail parties in New York and Washington. It was about the worst-kept secret around. What did they expect to happen?"

There was little or no coordination between Israeli and American Jewish officials with the network of Jewish-interest and Jewish-community newspapers and magazines in the United States. Editors of these journals received mixed signals from the Israeli government and the Jewish Agency, according to Jerome Lippman, coeditor of the *Long Island Jewish World*, and Gary Rosenblatt, editor of the *Baltimore Jewish Times*.

In Israel, explicit guidelines were given for handling the big story of the immigration of the Ethiopian Jews. The Israeli press—subject to the military censor on sensitive subjects, such as the situation of Jews in oppressed countries—had known about the secret for some time, and the editors of all eight Israeli dailies had agreed to keep the lid on the story. This was important even after the news of the airlift was published outside Israel, for there was a tacit agreement with Sudan and the various other parties involved in Operation Moses that Israel would not formally admit that the operation was going on.

On November 15, 1984, six days before the airlift was launched, the opening session of a congress of two thousand Jewish officials meeting in Toronto was broken up by a group of pro-Falasha activists led by Simcha Jacobovici, who had just published an article in the *New York Times*—an article that ran under the headline, "Ethiopian Jews Die, Israel Fiddles." A documentary film about the Falashas that Jacobovici had made earlier in the year featured an interview with a Sudanese government minister who said that the Jews in the camps were free to go, "no problem." This created a completely false impression of the reality in Sudan but gave credence to claims by American and Canadian activists that Israel and world Jewry were simply letting the Falashas die when they could have gotten them out.

At the Toronto General Assembly of the Council of

Jewish Federations, Jacobovici, holding an Ethiopian child in his arms, reiterated his view that Israel
could have saved the two thousand Jews who had died
in the camps that summer. His group carried signs
saying "Action Now" and "More Can Be Done." A
Jewish State Department official who was inti-
mately involved in Operation Moses and who was at
the meeting tried to persuade Jacobovici that something important was in the works and that he should
leave, but it was to no avail. The plenary session was
called off when it became impossible to appease the
demonstrators. Another State Department official
around the same time had pleaded with the board of
the American Association for Ethiopian Jews to keep
quiet because the airlift was about to be launched.
Although most AAEJ members acceded, at least one
of the leaders refused to believe the official.

At a subsequent session of the Toronto congress, the
head of the Jewish Agency, Arye (Leon) Dulzin, who
had found himself under attack for not doing enough
at a time when he knew the airlift was about to be
launched, felt that he had to at least allude to the secret. Dulzin, a longtime Zionist politician and a leader
of the business-oriented Liberal party, thereupon revealed that a secret operation was about to be
launched. In a speech to the assembled legions of
American and Canadian Jewish leaders, Dulzin said,
ironically, that any publicity would be ruinous and
swore everyone to secrecy. "When the true story of
the Jews of Ethiopia is told, we will take pride in what
we have already achieved in this most difficult and
complex rescue operation," he said.

What lifted the curtain completely was Dulzin's own
press release a few days after the Toronto congress,

following an address on November 20 to the World
Zionist Organization's American section meeting in
New York. The WZO press release was distributed
around the world by the Jewish Telegraphic Agency.
Dulzin did not mention the words Ethiopia, Sudan,
or airlift; but he did say that "an ingathering of an
historic, ancient community" and a "dramatic rise in
immigration" was in the works. A WZO official later
told the *Long Island Jewish World* that Dulzin was
given the opportunity to stop the press release but
decided to go ahead with it in order to help the UJA
fund-raising campaign, and perhaps to assuage the
critics.

The first paper anywhere to carry a story hinting
at the complex operation was the *Jewish Week* of Long
Island, a paper subsidized by the UJA New York federation. Its editor, David Gross, told me that American Jewish editors had been asked right after the
Toronto congress to keep everything about the rescue secret. But then came the Dulzin press release.
"That seemed to me to be a signal to publish something," Gross said.

Gross first consulted with national headquarters of
the United Jewish Appeal, got confirmation of its
Operation Moses fund-raising campaign, and decided to print the story. It appeared in the paper's
issue of November 23, 1984, two days after the airlift
had started. The story did not mention Sudan or use
the word airlift but said "a dramatic, mass rescue of
thousands of Ethiopian Jews and their transfer to Israel is scheduled to begin soon after January 1." It
quoted Dulzin as saying that although he was "not
free to discuss it publicly," preparations were under
way in Israel for "a sudden jump in immigration—

far beyond the figures we projected for the coming year." Dulzin added that "one of the ancient tribes of Israel is due to return to its homeland."

Gross defended his decision to publish. "An official release from the WZO *means* something; and there were no clear-cut guidelines." No one had had the wisdom to inform the editors of Jewish newspapers to keep completely silent, he said, maintaining that he himself had no misgivings about being the first to break the story. "We wrote a very cautious article, not mentioning the airlift. Only later did we get a call from the Israeli consulate asking us not to say anything at all," said Gross.

The *Washington Jewish Week*, a Jewish newspaper independent of the federations, put the rescue operation on the front page of its December 6 issue. The story, by Michael Berenbaum, announced that "the rescue of a substantial number of Ethiopian Jews has begun" and quoted his sources as government officials, Jewish professionals, and activists on behalf of Ethiopian Jews. He also quoted Dulzin's press release, adding that the UJA had launched a secret campaign to raise $60 million for the operation.

Berenbaum mentioned that the officials whom he and editor Charles Fenyevesi spoke to had cautioned them to keep the lid on. According to Fenyevesi, Israeli embassy officials as well as a lower-ranking State Department official had implored him not to mention the countries involved, the escape routes, or the scope of Operation Moses. He said he would have killed the story if someone "higher up" in the State Department had asked him to do so or if the officials had clearly stated that it was a matter of life or death.

Fenyevesi and Berenbaum went ahead "after carefully weighing the question," according to Berenbaum. Fenyevesi's editorial in the same issue as Berenbaum's report said "our obligation to inform the public" was the most important factor in deciding to run the story, "and it is hard to contain our joy in reporting that news." The story was "already known by too many people. It is only a matter of days before the press will come out with the dramatic details of the operation." The editorial added, incongruously, "We defer to the official requests for secrecy. Our hope is that one day soon we will publish the full story." But the damage that had started with Dulzin's statements had already begun to snowball.

Five days later, on December 11, the *New York Times* ran a page-one story citing the *Washington Jewish Week* article. The *Times* piece did not carry a byline but was written by Bernard Gwertzman, the Washington bureau's diplomatic correspondent. Gwertzman felt that the embargo was obviously off, since the Jewish media were reporting all but the details of the operation.

The story was carried on the *Times* national wire and picked up by most major newspapers. The day after the report, ABC News ran the story using footage of Ethiopian Jews in Israel.

The airlift reportedly was halted for only one flight immediately following the *New York Times* story, probably on Joshua's orders. But any delay at all was serious when lives were imperiled; in the camps the death toll from disease continued to be high. The Sudanese ignored the initial publicity, and the damage was contained. But the stage was set for further leaks.

Gross, of the *Long Island Jewish Week*, printed yet

another story about the rescue in the December 14
issue of his paper: "For several months reports have
been circulating in the American Jewish community
that a massive effort to rescue the Jews of Ethiopia
and bring them to Israel for permanent resettlement
was under way. Until this week, these reports were
either downplayed, denied or not commented upon
by responsible Jewish or Israeli leaders. This week,
however, following publication of the story on page
one of the *New York Times*, and more than two weeks
after *The Jewish Week* published a story, there are no
longer any denials." He went on to mention why a
lid was still on much of the information surrounding
the rescue effort—fears that it would be stopped "because of undue publicity."

Berenbaum, of the *Washington Jewish Week*, sub-
sequently admitted that there were many open questions, "including the propriety of our own role and
that of other newspapers." He was said later to be
upset and contrite about his part in the affair. Fenyevesi continued to defend publication of the story,
although he was aware of widespread revulsion in the
Jewish media and by Jewish officials and Israeli diplomats because of what was regarded as presump-
tuous "decision making" in a life-and-death situation.
Meanwhile, Dulzin—and Gross, for that matter—escaped the heat that was focused on Fenyevesi and his
editor, who had become the scapegoats.

One Israeli newspaper editor in chief who is
knowledgeable about the American Jewish media as
well as the Israeli press expressed support for Fenyevesi. "Charlie is a real newsman and his paper is
not tied to the Jewish federations. He doesn't accept
the usual bull associated with the Jewish organiza-

tion papers. Independent editors in Jewish journalism in America sometimes have to deal with an establishment that often seems overly conservative and as all-powerful as the Israeli establishment was in the 1950s, when you didn't have anything like a free press. It is unfair to make Fenyevesi and his reporter the scapegoats."

Fenyevesi told a reporter from the *Baltimore Jewish Times*, "Our job as journalists is to keep pressing. Their [Israel's and Jewish organization officials'] job is to say 'no,' but I didn't feel they were saying 'no' in the strongest terms they could have used, and I listened to my own conscience."

According to Robert Cohn, president of the American Jewish Press Association and editor of the *St. Louis Jewish Light*, Jewish newspapers responded to the secret operation in one of three ways: "There were those who said 'the hell with concerns about secrecy,' those who held out and didn't run any stories on the mission, and the vast majority who were completely baffled about how much, if any, to publish."

Gary Rosenblatt of the *Baltimore Jewish Times*, in a chronicle of how Operation Moses was suspended, pointed out that the UJA in early December 1984 was taking full-page ads in the Jewish papers appealing for donations to the rescue effort. (One such ad, in the *Los Angeles Jewish Bulletin*, said, "10,000 Ethiopian Jews can be rescued from starvation and persecution. This is an unparalleled moment in history. It is as if we could have saved 10,000 Jews from Auschwitz. . . .") Robert Cohn acknowledged that the editors were "getting mixed messages" from the Jewish Agency, the UJA, and the Israeli government. Rosenblatt suggested that the only way to prevent such a tragedy from happening again would be to inform the papers in advance. "Perhaps if the American Jewish newspapers had been apprised of the details of the rescue beforehand and told of the grave risks involved, the way the Jerusalem government briefed Israeli editors, there would have been a similar agreement to embargo the story."

Rosenblatt's newspaper commented editorially that the Jewish community had to think hard about how the operation was handled in terms of information and publicity. "As successful as the airlift itself was, that's how poorly the secret was kept." The newspaper quoted writer Elie Wiesel as saying, "Unfortunately, this is a case where the general press that we so often criticize handled itself more responsibly than a few of the Jewish newspapers. I don't understand how those Jewish editors could take the responsibility for endangering human lives."

But the publication of the story in no less a newspaper than the *New York Times* had turned out to mean very little indeed, as the *Boston Globe* gloated later. The Israeli papers continued to embargo the story, and this was the crucial factor as far as the Sudanese were concerned—it wasn't official. So the story died, even though the *Boston Globe* reported for the first time the pivotal role played by the U.S. government in acting as Israel's intermediary with the Sudanese.

As a result of the first news leak, the Israelis decided to accelerate the operation. On December 23, the flight rate was increased to once every twenty-four hours. Aleph had no more organizational troubles, and the operation had become almost routine. The Mossad agents were furious about Arye Dulzin's leaks and the media coverage but felt lucky that the damage had been limited.

More serious harm to the airlift was caused in the first days of 1985, with the publication of an interview with a Jewish Agency official by *Nekuda*, an obscure monthly put out by the Jewish settlers in the West Bank.

The hapless official, Yehuda Dominitz, had told the journal's reporter—off the record—that over half the tribe of Ethiopian Jews was already in Israel, a fact that was common knowledge among thousands of Israelis. Dominitz refused to comment on anything related to immigration operations. *Nekuda* wrote up the story, sensationalized it a bit, and, in defiance of regulations, did not submit it to the Israeli military censor. On January 3, 1985, Israel's two major morning tabloids, *Ma'ariv* and *Yediot Aharanot*, blew up the significance of Dominitz's statement and spread the story over several pages of their papers, illustrated by color photographs of Ethiopian Jews in Israel. The Associated Press and Reuters immediately picked up the story, and it went out to the world. That evening, after an interministerial committee discussed what to do, the government called an official press conference, in which Israeli officials tried to deflect attention to questions about the integration of Ethiopian Jews into Israeli society. "The real drama taking place now is their absorption in Israel," one Jewish Agency official told the assembled newsmen. But the calling of the press conference had in fact put an official stamp on the stories about the airlift. The Sudanese halted Operation Moses two days later, on January 5, 1985.

The news that thousands of Ethiopian Jews igno-

rant of the modern technological world were being
airlifted to Israel and into the twentieth century unleashed a flood of media attention in Israel. Newspapers went into great detail about the Ethiopians'
"primitive" origins and exotic diseases. The radio
played American black spirituals, with lines that must
have seemed cruelly ironic to those Ethiopian Jews
aware of the fact that their parents or children or
siblings still in Africa now faced an uncertain future
because of the news leaks: "Get on board little children / There's room for plenty more." Little discussion took place of the need for an inquiry into how
the story broke in the middle of the operation. Leaders of the Ethiopian Jewish community expressed
their fury over what they called a horrible botch, but
they were generally ignored.

In the censor's office, it was said that the story
"had" to come out sooner or later. The lid couldn't
be kept on, the censors maintained. One of them even
congratulated the Israeli press for exercising re-
straint for as long as it did and saw no reason to criticize the mass-circulation newspapers for running the
Nekuda story on their front pages. But the censors'
explanation simply wasn't credible; without a doubt,
a serious oversight had occurred within the censorship office.

The editors of *Nekuda* were not punished for their
violation. Politicians of the right-wing Tehiya party,
ideologically aligned with *Nekuda*, saw no reason to
criticize the settlers' organ and sought to put the
blame on Yisrael Peleg of the Government Press Office, who presided over the January 3 press conference. Foreign Minister Yitzhak Shamir, the Likud
leader, also blamed Peleg, a Labor party man. Shu-

lamit Aloni of the Citizens Rights Movement blamed
certain National Religious party members for encouraging the leak. (NRP leader Yosef Burg, the religious affairs minister, was known to have been
extremely reluctant to recognize the Falashas as Jews.)
Uzi Baram, Labor party secretary-general, blamed the
head of the Jewish Agency, Arye Dulzin, of the Likud's Liberal wing. And so on.

Once the *Nekuda* story was published, some people
asked why the censor, who had been so vigilant for
weeks, couldn't keep the story out of the media for a
few more days. Why did the government call its January 3 press conference, which finally made it official? It was difficult to pinpoint the blame, although
Prime Minister Peres assumed all responsibility for
the calling of the press conference. Some people felt
that it was the height of brazenness for Absorption
Minister Ya'acov Tsur to tell a television interviewer
that the UJA was to blame for the leaks. Unlike the
government, the UJA never officially confirmed Operation Moses.

Jewish Agency chairman Dulzin looked for the
brighter side. On January 4 a BBC interviewer asked
him if he regarded the news leak as a disaster. "I
wouldn't say a disaster," Dulzin opined. "I would say
it is a little risky. But I do believe that while the news
came out in the open, very few will dare to stop it
today, because it is such a great humanitarian operation that it would create an enormous scandal in the
world if somebody would dare stop it." The Sudanese stopped it the next day.

IN GEDAREF ON January 3, a Mossad agent informed
Aleph of the Israeli press conference but told him to

go ahead as if nothing had happened. Aleph made the arrangements for two more flights. But there would only be one more group of Jews flown from Khartoum, on Saturday night, January 5. The second group, Falashas from the Semien Mountains, had spent seven months in the camp at Maskar. They were contacted by relatives who had reached Gedaref town and met with Aleph. Aleph sent trucks to pick up 180 Jews in Maskar on January 6, 1985—but that's when the colonel in charge of the Sudanese side of the operation said, "No, the airlift is over."

Instead of going to Israel, the group was taken to Tuwawa. "We had no money, and in Tuwawa, you had to pay for food," one of the Semien Jews, Ephraim, told me. Several close relatives—including one of his brothers and a sister, who was the mother of four children—would die in the interim before the airlift could be completed.

In Israel on January 6, the Ethiopian Jews at the Ashkelon transit center bitterly assailed journalists who had been brought there by the Jewish Agency. They brandished fists and had to be physically restrained. One shouted at London *Times* correspondent Christopher Walker, "It is because of you that our families are suffering and may never get here." Another immigrant, who had been in Israel two months, said, "We just do not understand why the Israelis spoke out as they did about our escape. I have a father and brother still in Ethiopia, and I am afraid that now I will never see them again."

No one was certain how many Ethiopian Jews were stranded in the camps because of the news leaks, not even Aleph, who awaited developments while he holed up at the Gedaref safe house. Estimates in the press ranged from one thousand to three thousand. It was a diplomatic problem now, and top American officials, including President Reagan and Vice President Bush, put it on their agenda.

One State Department official in Washington was reluctant to talk to me about Operation Moses two weeks after the airlift was suspended because "leaks in the American Jewish press and from the Israeli government are costing Jewish lives. It is one of the great rescue stories of all time—heroic people went out there. Some were tortured and imprisoned. But it has all turned into a screwup. I can't understand the lack of control by the Jewish Agency and the Israeli government. The Israelis had told us that they were worried about *us* leaking!"

The State Department official, a key man in the planning of Operation Moses, said that he thought Arye Dulzin should be fired. "But the government press conference was by far the worst blunder in the whole affair." He said that he didn't understand "the pressures" on the Israeli government to call the press conference. "I went bananas when I heard about it. I think all of the leaks stem from the fact that everyone wants credit. I've seen the Israelis screw up a lot, but this is the worst, most tragic I've witnessed."

Like many others, he could not understand why the UJA fund-raising had to take place when it did. "We had thought that there would be no fund-raising until after the rescue operation was over. The State Department had that distinct impression. I appreciate that the UJA may have needed the drama for the fund-raising, but how could they do it? They didn't have to do it. The money was there."

7

Paying
for
It

The question
of why money had to be raised just as the airlift from
Sudan got under way understandably became a sensitive point with Israeli and American Jewish organization officials. The main fund-raising arm of U.S.
Jewry, the United Jewish Appeal, began its campaign for what it dubbed "Operation Moses" on November 27, 1984, six days after the leadership met in
New York with a top Israeli official, who had told
them that "a miracle" was in the process of unfold-

ing, that Israel was preparing to take all of the Jews out of Sudan and that the opportunity had just opened up. The official mentioned Israel's severe economic crisis and added, "We'll take the Falashas whether we can pay for it or not, but we need $60 million."

The UJA men questioned the official and told him that fund-raising would be difficult because of the constraints they would be working under. The official replied that they should not put anything into writing, just talk to people directly.

A day later, the UJA came up with a plan for the fund-raising. The world target was set at $82 million—$60 million from the UJA and $22 million from Keren Hayesod, the main Jewish fund-raising arm outside the United States. (Operation Moses funds were to be in addition to those raised in the 1985 UJA federation campaign.) A special Mailgram was sent to all communities that regularly raised over $3 million, inviting their top officials to a December 2 meeting in New York and setting a cash goal for each community.

Emergency meetings were scheduled throughout the nation in a slickly organized campaign that relied first on UJA regions and then on the individual federations and communities from Palm Springs to Palm Beach, from Minneapolis to Houston. It was an unprecedented peacetime campaign that reached not only the big donors but, through the nation's synagogues, the "new Jewish poor," the approximately one million American Jews who live below the poverty line or who are unemployed.

On November 28, two major donors who are UJA national vice chairmen, Martin Stein of Milwaukee and Alan Shulman of Palm Beach, together with UJA

vice president Elton Kerness, left for Israel to witness the Ethiopian rescue operation and report back.
Among some American Jewish leaders, the special
circumstances surrounding Operation Moses sparked
a more intensive appraisal of the UJA's relationship
with the Jewish Agency and the Israeli government.
They were aware that the fund-raising campaign, by
its very nature, jeopardized the actual operation—as
agency chairman Arye Dulzin had proven at the outset. One basic problem was the number of bodies involved: the government of Israel, the Jewish Agency,
the World Zionist Organization, Keren Hayesod, and
the UJA. Guidelines from the Israelis were lacking.

When I went to New York to cover the UJA campaign aspect of Operation Moses in mid-January 1985,
I was immediately confronted by a leadership with
its back up, including Stanley Horowitz, president of
UJA; Vice President Kerness; and Assistant Vice
President for Communications Rafi Rothstein. Horowitz, a meticulous UJA professional, said he was
sorry that I had come all the way from Israel, because they were not going to cooperate. "No meetings with reporters, we've decided. Lives are at stake.
What is there to gain by talking to the press? We have
been put in a tough situation, asked to raise a great
deal of money, and to do so without publicity. I believe we've been very responsible." In the light of all
the leaks, Horowitz said, he had become "gun-shy."
But he changed his mind on condition that nothing
would be published until it was safe to do so.

Had the UJA men questioned the basic concept
of raising funds just as the operation was being
launched? Couldn't Israel have borrowed $20 mil-
lion or so from a bank, or taken it from the defense
budget? "Of course it bothered us," Horowitz admit-

ted. "We had a plan for raising funds in the future, after the operation." Israel's request came at a time when the UJA leaders were meeting on Israel's general economic problem. "Maybe if the economic situation had been healthier," Horowitz said, "we would have waited."

The UJA leaders expressed pride in their highly organized network of associated federations that enabled them to mount a major operation and yet keep it relatively quiet. "It was incredible how much was done without the written word," Horowitz said. "We've tied our own hands. The American Jewish community has performed brilliantly."

According to Kerness, no one on the Israeli side even hinted that the fund-raising might impede Operation Moses, "no one said there was a risk." In addition, he said, "if we waited until afterward, until everyone had reached Israel, it would have been much harder to raise the funds. We felt it was better to do it now. Many of us thought that there might be a backlash because the Beta-Israel are black—but the color question never arose. We needed the drama factor, the message that we are saving their lives."

The "lay leaders" of the UJA—big donors who are not Jewish-organization officials—were generally uncritical of the Israeli request to raise money concurrently with the airlift. Bob Loup, a Denver real estate man who chairs the UJA Board of Trustees, has been known as one of the most outspoken UJA leaders. But he defended the decision and criticized his local federation newspaper, the *Intermountain Jewish News*—"which had previously been very responsible"—for questioning the Jewish Agency's judgment in starting the campaign when it did. Loup, who is also a member of the agency's Board of Governors,

said, "The Israel government is broke, pure and simple—there was nowhere to get the money." Loup did
express disappointment with the way the Israel government handled the publicity of Operation Moses—
specifically the leaks and the government's press
conference, which had forced the airlift to be interrupted. He felt that the UJA shouldn't have to be the
scapegoat for Israeli blunders.

Steven Grossman, a Boston man active in the UJA's
Young Leadership, also maintained that the fund-
raising had not been started prematurely. "The money
had to be raised right now. Without the emergency,
it might not have been possible."

But the controversy over the timing of the campaign did leave a residue of doubt among some of the
top UJA fund-raisers, who have become less than
comfortable with the organization's intimate association with the Jewish Agency, which administers most
of the money raised for Israel. When UJA representatives on missions to Israel get off the beaten track
and talk with Israelis in their homes, they find that
the Jewish Agency is widely criticized, that many Israelis question its very existence, contending that it
is a wasteful, unnecessary bureaucracy. But, at least
for the record, most UJA leaders defended the agency,
maintaining that it is run as well as can be expected
in an often inefficient Israel.

IN THE FIRST week of the UJA campaign, a group of
five Israelis was flown in to speak to gatherings of the
major donors. Yehuda, who was the only Ethiopian
Jew among them, was introduced to audiences as "Mr.
X." He spoke on only two occasions before he was
called back suddenly, to help deal with a snag in the

Sudan operation. Rina, his wife, took over, and soon proved to be the UJA's most dynamic speaker. The stocky Israeli social worker from Jerusalem took to the circuit like a combination of Elmer Gantry and Golda Meir. "She was a natural," one UJA official said.

The members of the Israeli mission were given a UJA packet entitled "Operation Moses: Leadership Briefing Portfolio" full of secondhand information about the Ethiopian Jews, but were left on their own as to what to say. At the first Operation Moses meeting on December 2, two hundred UJA leaders—staff-members and the major donors—from across the country met at the Sheraton–La Guardia Hotel in New York. It was at this meeting that the basic plan was completed by the representatives of the thirty-seven major communities and five regions. One slogan they adopted said that the $60 million was needed "to rescue ten thousand Ethiopian Jews." In actuality, the money was to help finance the initial resettlement costs for Ethiopian Jews, but "rescue" was seen as a much more exciting cause. Alex Grass, national chairman, opened the session by emphasizing the urgency of the project. He was followed by Jewish Agency immigration official Yehuda Dominitz, and then by Rina. She spoke touchingly, describing how the new immigrants were arriving, and saying that these people were part of her family and nothing less. She also tried to drive home the importance of keeping the operation secret. (The story would break nine days later.) Rina concluded by saying that American Jews had a historic opportunity to give the gift of life to "a noble Jewish tribe."

In the swirl of meetings that followed, Rina often brought her audiences to tears with a slightly exag-

gerated, lachrymose, but essentially accurate view of
the great distress suffered by the Ethiopian Jews. She
was capable of being much more objective, more
critical, but this wasn't the time or place. One still
had to "sell" the idea of the Ethiopian Jews to the
other Jews in the world, she believed.

Rina was stunned by the spirit that pervaded the
meetings. Whenever she described the bedraggled but
regal appearance of the Beta-Israel and how they
kissed the ground of Israel when they arrived, her
voice cracked, and many in the audience were moved
to tears. It appeared that something far beyond
"checkbook Judaism" was happening.

FOR AMERICAN JEWRY in general, there had never been
anything quite like it. The deliverance of Ethiopian
Jews was the best news out of Israel in many years,
and it struck some deep chords in the country with
the biggest Jewish population in the world. It came
at a time when black-Jewish relations in America were
severely strained and when the Jewish community
itself was divided over support for Israel on the Lebanon war, settlement in the West Bank and Gaza
territories, and the contentious issue of "Who is a
Jew?" (Israel's Orthodox parties periodically pro-
pose an amendment to the 1950 Law of Return that
would exclude Jews converted by Reform or Conservative rabbis—who represent the majority of
American Jews.) Ethiopian Jews saw their rescue in
miraculous terms; secular Israelis saw it as part of
the Zionist idea, what Israel is all about. But for many
American Jews, relations with the black community
were an important added element.

American Jews and blacks have been closely linked

since the Roosevelt era and continue to be so, de-spite the sharp differences that have emerged be-tween the two minority communities. The erosion that began in the 1960s has accelerated in recent years. The revelation that black Jews living in the Horn of Africa were threatened, and that Israel was going all out to extricate them, was a positive development for those who have been trying to bridge the gap be-tween the two communities. In Boston, the UJA's Steven Grossman said that the rescue operation "can only help to rebuild the traditional coalition be-tween blacks and Jews—and I think it's very impor-tant that it be rebuilt. We have common shared values on questions of basic social justice."

Relations between Jews and blacks have deterio-rated since the New York City school strike in 1968 set Jews and blacks against each other. An appalling amount of racial prejudice surfaced in both commu-nities. Job competition, envy, and fear began to dominate relations between many blacks and Jews, and the Israeli-Arab conflict further polarized the two communities. In 1979, a storm arose over UN am-bassador Andrew Young's meeting with a PLO rep-resentative. The Jewish leadership, tipped off by Israel, eventually played a major part in forcing Young to resign, which set off a backlash among blacks. It was all seen as a metaphor for a struggle between competing ethnic groups.

Dr. Kenneth Clark, delving into the background of the increasing friction, said that Jews seem to talk more about ethics and morality than any other white group, and so blacks "tend to expect more from Jews." Jesse Jackson's candidacy for the 1984 Democratic presidential nomination widened the gulf, though

black congressmen continued to support U.S. aid to
Israel, and most Jewish congressmen still backed civil
rights legislation and affirmative action.

When the Falasha story broke in January 1985, both
communities suddenly were called upon to raise their
consciousness about black-Jewish relations. American blacks have traditionally identified with the Israelites of the Bible, and it appeared that some of
them now began to rethink their relationship to the
Jews of today and to Israel. They may still have believed that the Palestinians had a genuine grievance
that would have to be settled one day, but it would
be difficult to question the appropriateness of Israel
as the new home for *these* Jews—a persecuted and
impoverished black African people with ancient Jewish roots.

A few days after the story hit the headlines, Clar-
ence Walter, a black New Yorker and born-again
Christian, offered a man-in-the-street reaction to Operation Moses: "These are very exciting times—Ethiopian Jews, why, that's right out of the Bible,
prophecy. Bringing in that lost tribe is one of the great
events of our time."

Many blacks who oppose Israel's policies were
either silent or condemned the operation, contending that Israel took the Ethiopians just because they
would provide cheap labor. Black friends of Israel
were enthusiastic and welcomed the rescue. Bill Tatum, publisher-editor of the *Amsterdam News*, the
leading black newspaper in America, said, "Israel
should be praised for saying that 'this black tribe is
the Tribe of Dan, and I want my brother home.' "

In an interview near his newspaper's Harlem office, Tatum noted that the black-Jewish relationship

in the United States remains very strong and that
Operation Moses would reinforce the ties. In practical terms, that spelled continued support for Israel
by most black political leaders.

He criticized the oil-rich Arab countries for only
paying lip service to the principle of aid for the dis-
tressed African masses. He said that even America
would never do what Israel had done, taking in fourteen thousand black refugees. "The U.S. refugee quota
for all Africa—including North and South Africa—is
less than three thousand people per year," Tatum remarked. "I'm heartened by what Israel has done."

He felt that the way American Jews had responded
to Operation Moses would be interpreted affirma-
tively by American blacks. "It is a real opportunity
to increase awareness of the bonds that tie us together, a meeting ground between the traditions of
Judaism and of Africa. I see it as a healthy development." Tatum, who is married to a Jew, said that his
thirteen-year-old daughter was overjoyed by Operation Moses and hungered for more information about
the Ethiopian Jews.

Author John A. Williams, who had written a play
about the need to rescue the Ethiopian Jews, was one
of a number of black intellectuals who praised Israel's action and said that it would help bring American Jews and blacks closer together. "I can say
without any reservations—it is good news. Israel came
through, just in time." But he was upset about the
way the Israeli and American media treated the subject: "Whatever has been presented has been in the
style of the Wolf Boy brought into civilization. Is he
gonna make it?" Williams also expressed concern for
those Jews who were left behind in Ethiopia.

IN RECENT YEARS American Jews have developed a great sensitivity to criticism that American Jewry did not do enough during World War Two to spur the U.S. government to save European Jews in Nazi-satellite countries such as Hungary and Romania. "Holocaust guilt" would become a constant theme in Operation Moses fund-giving events and propaganda. Many Jewish leaders would say, "We can do now what we couldn't do in the 1940s," or, "We should have done more in the 1940s, now we can make up for it." The "Never Again" syndrome was strong in Los Angeles, for example. "We heard a great deal of talk at the fund-raising events about how European Jews were not saved during the Holocaust and that this must not occur again," said Erwin Levin of the local federation. "Everyone wanted an 'I Saved a Life' button." Which they got for six thousand dollars.

Marty Stein, the forty-seven-year-old pharmacist who in addition to being national vice chairman of UJA is president of the Milwaukee Jewish Federation, had seen the actual airlift in Israel a week after it began. When he entered the plane in the military section of the airport, his thoughts were of the Yad Vashem Holocaust Memorial in Jerusalem, "of pictures of the Auschwitz survivors—gaunt faces, huge eyes staring back at me." Bob Loup, of Denver, also thought of Auschwitz and "the chance to save Jewish babies." In their emotional reactions to Operation Moses, many American Jews felt that the similarities between the situation of the Ethiopian Jews and that of the European Jews under Hitler gave added impetus to the intense fund-raising efforts.

The whole structure of organized Jewish life was

called into action for Operation Moses. Some two
hundred autonomous Jewish federations are linked
in this UJA network, with the purpose of distributing
Jewish philanthropic funds. The local groups are run
according to their own methods, drawing on the national organization for speakers, missions, and guidance. But the fundamental responsibility is with the
local entities. They use their own judgment in many
ways, playing a part in a national objective, but with
their own programs.

By the end of January, scores of fund-raising meetings were being held throughout the country, with the
nonprofessional leaders swinging into action. Marty
Stein was considered one of the most effective speakers. In one month, he spoke at thirty meetings around
the country, from small dinner affairs of a dozen major givers to audiences of five hundred, telling them
that "we have an opportunity to save people. We have
to give till it hurts." (Stein himself was one of the
biggest donors, pledging $240,000 to the general UJA
campaign, including $30,000 for Operation Moses.) He
told his audiences to "get involved, to stand up and
be counted, to get your grandchildren involved in this
wonderful event happening in the community."

"We've raised more money and done it faster for
Operation Moses than in past campaigns," said Alex
Grass, the top lay person at UJA. The $60 million
would just be for starters: Israeli government officials were already estimating that absorption costs
would soon reach $300 million. Twelve hundred or-
phans were among the Ethiopian immigrants, Grass
noted. That meant much more expensive care. Family units were also smaller than originally projected—perhaps because of the high death toll on the

trek out of Ethiopia and in the refugee camps. "And that means that more apartments are required."

Elton Kerness had been No. 2 at UJA for only six months before Operation Moses was thrown in his lap. The lay leaders of the UJA gave him much of the credit for the success of the campaign. Kerness felt that American Jews identified closely with Israel's action because "no black nation has done what Israel did; no Moslem country took in black Moslem refugees; no Christian country took in Christian Ethiopians. American Jews have been giving to the Ethiopian relief effort as a whole while at the same time taking care of their own people." He felt this was an answer to all the outspoken pro-Falasha activists in North America: "The minute we had the opportunity to get them out, we did it."

OPERATION MOSES HAD a dramatic impact on American rabbis, according to Rabbi Stanley Kessler, chairman of the UJA's Rabbinic Cabinet, a council of 180 of the nation's leading rabbis. It was holding its annual meeting in Washington just as Operation Moses was launched. Kessler called this a "divine coincidence." State Department officials Eugene Douglas and Princeton Lyman, key figures in the initiating of Operation Moses, spoke to the council's opening session. The rabbis pledged $75,000 of their own money, then went back to their home communities "and did tremendous fund-raising."

A rabbi in Sacramento, California, spoke from the pulpit and told his congregants that he had just given $1,000 and that they should follow suit. "Thirty members did just that," Kessler said. Another rabbi in New York raised $250,000 after one sermon.

By involving the rabbis, "you got the electricity going; such involvement is unprecedented," said Rabbi Richard Davis, UJA's director of the Rabbinic Cabinet. "It was a unique situation. They couldn't rely on the printed word. Jews were reached through the synagogues."

Letters from rabbis poured in every day. Money came from some Orthodox synagogues that had never raised money for the UJA before. Many synagogues took an "adopt a *minyan*" approach, with a goal of raising $60,000. (A *minyan* is the minimum number of adult Jewish males required for Jewish public worship—ten—and $6,000 was the amount set "to save one life.") "Virtually every synagogue in the United States is doing something in Operation Moses," Rabbi Davis said.

The UJA kept a low profile with student groups, feeling that student newspapers by their very nature would "not be discreet"—a somewhat ironic observation, given the indiscretions of "grown-up" Jewish officials and newspapers. But in December 1984 the UJA took 150 student leaders to Israel to visit Ethiopian Jews at the Beersheba absorption center and a youth village near Haifa. The students raised $19,000, compared with $10,000 for the entire UJA campaign the previous year.

THE UJA RAISED most of its money in intimate get-togethers, and the very best results came from one-on-one meetings with big donors. The largest grants were $500,000 from a Los Angeles man, two $300,000 donations from Baltimore, and a number of $250,000 donations from New York. Many of the gifts were for $6,000 or multiples of that figure.

A typical fund-raising event was held in late January 1985 at a synagogue in Short Hills, New Jersey, a prosperous suburban town about fifty miles from New York City. The Jewish population of Metrowest, the three north Jersey counties of the region, is 110,000, 26,000 of whom contribute to the UJA. The target for Operation Moses was set at $1.5 million, more than half of which had already been raised in previous events.

The twenty-four rabbis in the area had written to all their congregants, and, according to Marty Neier, one of the local federation officials, the reaction was "super." The synagogues were sending in a steady stream of checks, including some three thousand individual donations ranging from $5 to $24,000. "People who normally give $25 were giving $500."

The Short Hills meeting of the UJA's "country club division" took place at Bnai Jeshuran congregation, the largest Reform synagogue in the area, where four Jewish country clubs are located, all of which had become involved in Operation Moses. Bnai Jeshuran, a sprawling redbrick synagogue, itself looks like a country club. Herman Lebersfeld, the Operation Moses chairman for the Metrowest area, had visited Ethiopian Jews at a transit center in Ashkelon and thought, "This is what Israel is all about." He felt that it was important to impart the excitement to his own community.

Kenneth Rempell, a South Orange businessman who was one of the most active lay leaders in Metrowest and a member of the national UJA Young Leadership, also was greatly moved during the Metrowest leaders' visit to the new immigrants. Potentially, the Ethiopian *aliyah* could become important in raising Jewish consciousness in America, he believed. Upon his return to the United States, he talked to groups of ninth and tenth graders about the historic importance of the Ethiopian migration and found that their knowledge was virtually nil.

According to Adele Lebersfeld, who headed the women's division of the UJA campaign, "Our twelve thousand members raised one-sixth of the campaign money. A lot of the women in our community don't work; they have more time and get the husbands involved as well." Sandy Greenburg, vice president of the women's division, interjected that women are the ones who "get emotional, and the men get involved because of their wives."

In the auditorium of the synagogue, the first speaker, Avram Gannet, told the gathering of about sixty people that it was courageous of Israel to undertake Operation Moses at a time of severe economic crisis. Now it was up to American Jews. "We must help our Ethiopian Jewish brothers and sisters. Our share of the $60 million is $1.5 million. Many of you have already made gifts. We're asking for more. The operation must be paid for before March 31. We've already sent $800,000 to Israel. It is an appeal that goes to the root of what Israel is all about—saving lives."

Gannet also tried to convey to the audience how inspiring it was to witness the arrival of the Ethiopians in Israel. The Americans had been impressed by the efforts of the social workers striving to reduce the anxiety of the refugees. "We were mesmerized by the quiet dignity of the Ethiopian Jews, the way they all sat silently before eating, their demeanor. Some had Coptic mohawk-type haircuts so that they could

pass as Christians in the Sudan camps. Five-year-old
kids looked like they were two because they were so
malnourished."

He talked of the immigrants' "incredibly intense
desire for learning" and how the youngsters read into
the night—always a crowd pleaser for Jewish audiences. "We have to raise not only our own consciousness but that of the world. This population is black
but Jewish. In Israel, they've been received with open
arms. We all know about the black-Jewish controversy from the last election. I think we can be proud
for taking in blacks, and blacks will recognize this.
It also makes a sham out of the Zionism-equals-rac-
ism slur. This is a great chapter in Jewish history."

Marty Neier distributed pledge cards to the audience and asked them to think in terms of multiples
or fractions of $6,000. When pledge time came around,
the Lebersfelds started off. "We pledge $6,000 to save
one life." The Rempells also pledged $6,000. Another
man and his family followed suit. One elderly man
who had asked, "How Jewish are they, really?" also
pledged $6,000. A young man stood up and said that
he had originally pledged $100 but would now give
$600: "Instead of a memorial in Israel, we have a liv-
ing people to give to." After some $70,000 had been
raised, Adele Lebersfeld wound up the comments,
saying, "I'm overwhelmed by what's happening, very
emotional. Why didn't we do more in 1942 to help
European Jews escape? I know I'll be able to tell my
grandchildren what we've done now, in 1985."

One of the reasons the national UJA leadership had
been reluctant to open their operations to journalists
was because of the temptation to satirize the fund-
raising activities. It was known that some of the lo-

cal federations would be overly enthusiastic—to put
it graciously—in raising funds. For example, one
temple on Long Island, Congregation Etz Chaim, sent
a letter to all its members on January 7, 1985, saying
that "10,000 Ethiopian Jews are in the Sudan and
must be rescued or they will fall into the hands of
the PLO." But despite the occasional ridiculous speech
or flier, it was clear that a great deal of goodwill prevailed. After years of either ignoring the issue or being
ignorant of it, organized American Jewry had come
to accept the Ethiopian Jews as their brothers and
sisters.

News of the operation was a great lift for American Jews, "coming after Lebanon, West Bank controversy, the economic mess—all of which caused
divisiveness in the Jewish community, although not
from a fund-raising aspect," said Steven Grossman,
who, together with his father, Edgar, headed the UJA
campaign in the Greater Boston area. The Gross-
mans had sharp differences between themselves over
the building of settlements in Judea and Samaria, for
example, but Operation Moses "transcended all of
this. It has given American Jewry a magnificent opportunity to rescue Jews, to perform a religious duty,
express solidarity, show the finest the Jewish people
have to offer. No one has questioned this moral imperative," said Grossman.

What Grossman found most striking was that Operation Moses was the first Israeli event other than a
war that was "bringing Jews here together—an issue
that people want not only to give money to but actually to participate in. At last, we have an issue on
which we can all unite."

Grossman was one of the many local UJA lay leaders who went to Israel to see the treatment the Ethiopian new immigrants were receiving. On a visit to a tuberculosis ward at the aptly named Sheba Hospital, Grossman's translator, an Ethiopian who had been in Israel for a year, came across his newly arrived four-year-old nephew. "Scenes like this one made Operation Moses more real to me; it helped to bring it all back home. Previously, before I had ever met an Ethiopian Jew, I had felt detached, didn't sense the urgency of the situation, and felt much more connected to the problem of Soviet Jews."

In general, one found highly intelligent and well-motivated people involved in the UJA efforts. They have been much underrated, dismissed as corny by nonestablishment Jews in the United States; taken for granted or entirely ignored by Israeli Jews. By any standards, their participation in Operation Moses was a noble achievement by American Jews.

8

Operation Sheba

Throughout Operation Moses, Jewish travelers visited the area around Gondar in the Ethiopian highlands, where several thousand Falashas remained. Barry Weise, an official of the National Jewish Community Relations Advisory Council, the umbrella group for all American Jewish community relations organizations, organized and led several missions to Ethiopia. In November 1984, the month the airlift began, Weise brought seventeen people with the cooperation of the

171

Ethiopian government. He believed the government
allowed the visit because it was seeking to rebuild the
tourist industry, which once added about $200 mil-
lion a year to the economy. "They also wanted to show
that there was religious freedom, that the restrictions on the Jews had been eased."

The next month, another group, sponsored by the
North American Conference on Ethiopian Jewry and
headed by activist Barbara Ribicave, took two missions to Ethiopia to attend the Falashas' Seged celebration. They found that although the famine had not
yet devastated the Gondar region, the price of grain
had tripled. The traditional feast marking the end of
the Seged was modest and low keyed.

The American groups visited some Jewish villages
south of Ambover, where they heard reports of attacks against the Jews—women raped, synagogues
stripped, mud-wattle houses taken over. "Because so
few young men are left to defend the villages, they
remain very vulnerable," Weise said. He did not believe that the attacks were government-inspired. "It
could be much worse for the remaining Jews, as
they're considered traitors to Ethiopia. They were all
ready to leave and didn't plant full fields after hearing of the escape route through Sudan." He esti-
mated that as many as ten thousand Jews remained
in Ethiopia.

In January 1985, when the airlift became a major
news story worldwide, an Israeli journalist, Amos
Elon, had no trouble visiting Ambover village. He
traveled as a tourist and did not identify himself as
a newsman. Ambover, once the center of activity for
the great majority of the Ethiopian Jews, was more
than half-empty, with only a handful of young peo-

ple remaining. Another journalist who visited Ambover in February reported that only three hundred
heads of family were left, compared with over one
thousand previously. Many more women than men
were in the villages—widows with small children, and
the elderly. Many of those who remained were too old
or infirm to travel. But even after the story broke,
groups of Ethiopian Jews were still defying the government, leaving the village at night and heading west
toward the Sudan border.

The security situation of the remaining Jews started
to become much more precarious by mid-February
of 1985. Two Ethiopian guides who accompanied
American senators to one of the villages in the north
were punched and kicked by five state security police officers and accused of being CIA agents. Vir-
ginia senator Paul Trible, Jr., and Arizona senator
Dennis DeConcini said later that the treatment of the
two guides suggested that security could not be
guaranteed for the remaining Ethiopian Jews. They
appealed to the Ethiopian government to permit the
Jews to emigrate freely in order to be reunited with
their families in Israel and elsewhere.

"We indicated that people in America and other
countries were concerned about the fate of the Falashas," Senator Trible said, "and that if the government of Ethiopia would take action, there would be
a very positive response which would enhance our
relations."

Other American legislators, such as Congressman
Gary L. Ackerman of Queens, New York, who also
visited the Gondar area in February 1985, emphasized to the Ethiopians that improved relations with
the United States might depend on human rights

questions such as the reunification of Jewish families. Some government officials in Addis Ababa responded that they would "seriously consider" appeals
on behalf of the Jews; but the calls were just as likely
to have a boomerang effect—the Ethiopians have not
taken kindly to criticisms leveled by democratic
countries or by human rights organizations such as
Amnesty International. It should be recalled that
Ethiopia's estrangement from the United States accelerated because of former president Jimmy Cart-
er's human rights policy. Washington cut off military
aid in the late 1970s in reaction to Ethiopia's hard-
line position on civil liberties, so the Ethiopians went
to Moscow for arms. Mengistu once dismissed Western claims of "abuse" of human rights, pointing out
that "these same countries not only shamelessly kept
silent in the face of the immense violation of human
rights which were prevalent under the defunct feudal regime, but also actively encouraged and supported them."

In the wake of Operation Moses, the Dergue was not
about to "seriously consider" any appeals concerning the Jews. Indeed, the country's leadership charged
that the Falashas were kidnapped "in a sinister operation" and taken to Israel against their will. The
communist party line was that the Falashas were not
Jews at all, and Marxist Ethiopian professors were
sent around the world to spread the word.

The Ethiopian government did not cooperate with
Israel in any way, according to both Israeli and
American officials. The Israeli authorities said this in
public, as might be expected, and in private as well.
At the January 3, 1985, press conference in Jerusa-
lem called by the government after the airlift story

broke, Moshe Gilboa, head of the Foreign Ministry desk dealing with Ethiopian Jewry, said that no *quid pro quo* had been given to the Ethiopian government.

For weeks after the disclosure of the airlift, Sudan and Ethiopia swapped charges over which of them had "colluded with the Zionists." Addis Ababa complained about an Israeli-Sudanese conspiracy against Ethiopia; Khartoum assailed an Israeli-Ethiopian-Libyan conspiracy against the Sudanese, Eritrean, Palestinian, and Somali peoples. In Israel, it was feared that the hundreds of Jews stranded in the Sudan might have to endure the deathly refugee camps for many months, until things cooled down.

In Addis Ababa on January 15, 1985, Goshu Wolde, the foreign minister of Ethiopia, condemned Sudan for attempting to hide "its obvious complicity in the illegal trafficking of Ethiopian nationals to Israel." Goshu charged that Sudan, "which is currently engaged in a widespread massacre of the indigenous African inhabitants of southern Sudan," was blatantly interfering in Ethiopia's internal affairs. He dismissed Sudan's allegations that Israel had transferred to Ethiopia large quantities of Palestinian arms captured in the Lebanon war as an attempt to create a wedge between Revolutionary Ethiopia and the Palestinian people, and that Ethiopia had long used the Falashas as a bargaining card for obtaining more arms and money through the Israeli Amiran Company, which has an office in Addis Ababa.

(Israel did in fact give aid to Ethiopia during the famine, but this was humanitarian relief: tons of flour, sugar, baby food, edible oil, ten field kitchens, hundreds of tents, and large quantities of medicine.

Also, private Israelis, such as peace activist Abie Nathan, built tent cities for non-Jewish Ethiopian refugees. Similar aid was sent by Israel's "Red Cross," Magen David Adom, to famine victims in Kenya and other countries hit by the drought.)

The Ethiopian response to Operation Moses was encapsulated by Colonel Mengistu in an interview with the Canadian Broadcasting Corporation soon after the airlift was disclosed, in which he described it as a forcible abduction of Ethiopians. The usually media-shy leader called it "indirect slavery" and said that the Falashas reaching Israel were committing suicide in droves. (A total of eight suicides of Ethiopians who had immigrated since 1980 had been reported up to that time—not a large number given the trauma of their escape, the rescue, and adjustment to a new world.)

Mengistu said that the Falashas were not Jews and that Israel brought them only because it had "collected" Jews from all over the world but had none to represent black Africa. "This act is illegal and inhuman. They have been forced to go there [to Israel] against their wish, and, as such, we want them back in their native land."

Mengistu, like the emperors before him, often has expressed his commitment to unity as his government's fundamental principle. "Above all, the unity of Ethiopia will be the sacred faith of our people," he once said. Everyone in Ethiopia "belongs" to Ethiopia, and the battle cry of the revolution has been "Ethiopia First." His predecessor, Haile Selassie, once told Jewish visitors that the departure of the entire Falasha tribe would be "a national disaster," and perhaps Mengistu felt that way too—not because of the modest numbers involved but because of its symbolic importance. In January 1985 Ethiopia registered a formal complaint at the United Nations against Israel for "abducting" Ethiopian refugees.

Hebrew University Professor Olga Kapuliuk, an internationally recognized authority on revolutionary Ethiopia who is generally sympathetic to the Marxist regime, does not attach much significance to Mengistu's professions about the "abduction" of the Falashas. The Beta-Israel are such a minuscule percentage of Ethiopia's population that nobody really cares if they leave or not, she told me. Her impression from a visit to Ethiopia in December 1984, during the airlift, was that the government "did not mind" if people left the famine-stricken, overpopulated areas, and might even have encouraged the exodus of refugees from the northern provinces into Sudan. Mengistu and the military committee that rules Ethiopia command an army of 300,000 well-equipped men. They could easily have stopped the Falashas and anyone else from getting out, she maintained.

Another Israeli authority on Ethiopia, Professor Hagai Ehrlich of Tel Aviv University's Shiloah Institute, also believed that the exodus of so small a number of people was insignificant to the Ethiopians: "They didn't care as long as it was all under the table and not an open campaign of 'Let my people go.' " In the long run, he said, Ethiopia needs Israel, and Mengistu knows this. "We're not considered enemies but potential allies. So although they have made a lot of fuss verbally, in practical terms it's all very minor to them."

But Dr. Steven Kaplan, a history scholar who heads the Beta-Israel research project at the Ben-Zvi Institute in Jerusalem, offered a different view. "The

Ethiopian government's most important issue is national unity. It overshadows the drought, as was shown by the fact that famine relief was withheld from rebel areas. The Falasha issue strikes at the very heart of the unity question; here is a people saying that they are not Ethiopians. Mengistu's anger was genuine."

Professor Kapuliuk suggests that the sharp Ethiopian reaction to Operation Moses stemmed from the fact that the Dergue has tried to prove that no racial or ethnic discrimination is allowed to exist in Socialist Ethiopia. "They are very sensitive about this point." She said that the waves of persecution and arrests of Falashas trying to get out occurred only because they were seen as "foreign agents." Any connection between a national minority and a foreign power engendered a great deal of suspicion in Ethiopia, as it would in any other country.

After Operation Moses, fears mounted for the safety of the remaining Jews in Ethiopia following reports that the Dergue had decided to solve the "Falasha problem" by breaking up Jewish villages and dispersing the Beta-Israel to the malarial lowlands in the southwest. Some two thousand Jews from the Lasta region, where the Falashas have suffered the worst persecutions, were scheduled to be the first to be "resettled." Such resettlement could mean the end of the Beta-Israel's communal life and a weakening of the religious observance that has been the core of their identity for so many centuries.

About three hundred Ethiopian Jews remained in Addis Ababa. Some of them—educated and relatively well assimilated—sought to immigrate to Canada. Others were desperate to rejoin their spouses or children or parents in Israel. Previous arrangements

for getting Jews out—through scholarships or adop-
tion—were no longer operative, and the prospects for
their emigration had narrowed considerably after
Operation Moses.

At least three private non-Israeli Jewish groups still
actively tried to get these Jews out. But the best-
funded of the groups reportedly laid down a proviso
that it would help only those Jews who wanted to go
to Israel. They were demanding "Israel or else" for
the Falashas, practicing a narrow kind of Zionism that
some Jews have also applied to Soviet Jewry.

One Israeli official, a man whose interest in the Falashas flagged considerably after he had been among
those who accepted the applause for Operation Moses,
told me that he believed that only five thousand Jews
were left in Ethiopia, not ten thousand. "Besides the
elderly and the sick, many simply do not want to
come," he asserted. Indeed, the situation of the Jews
in Ethiopia no longer appeared to be a top priority
for at least some Israeli officials who subscribed to
this appraisal. However, others associated with Operation Moses said that it might still be possible to
bring several thousand more Ethiopian Jews to Israel if the once-good relations with the Addis Ababa
regime could be restored.

Yehuda, who had been involved in Operation Moses
from the beginning, was not sanguine about the
chances for those who remained. He sounded coldly
realistic when he told a friend: "In Ethiopia, only a
few hundred are left as far as we're concerned. They'll
get out one way or another. The rest know that they
will never make it to Israel. We know that too."

FOR THE MOST part, Israel's action won plaudits around
the world, with the obvious exceptions of the Soviet

bloc, the Arab world, and some leftist elements. A diplomat at the Foreign Ministry in Jerusalem said that he was most pleased with the positive reactions coming out of the Third World, where Israel's rescue operation was generally described as imaginative and humanitarian. The Nairobi daily newspaper *Sunday Nation*, which often follows an anti-Israel line, was one of several African papers that lauded Operation Moses. It said that Israel had carried out a righteous act despite the country's hyper-inflation and an economy in ruins. The newspaper, noting that Israel had "decided to take care of its own in Ethiopia," asked, "Doesn't Africa have a conscience too?"

Many African leaders, speaking in private, praised Operation Moses and said that it was the biggest boost to Israel's image since the rescue of hostages at Entebbe in 1976. Donations to help the Ethiopian Jews poured into Jerusalem from Jews and gentiles all over the world.

In the United States, newspapers and magazines hailed the exodus from Sudan. *Time* magazine was notably sympathetic, although its reporting was not completely accurate. *Time* said that "prior to the present airlift, the typical method of escape was for couriers, financed mainly by private American Jewish organizations, to smuggle Falashas into Israel in small groups." That was the impression conveyed by the AAEJ in its self-publicity and in a well-covered celebration it held in Israel after the completion of the airlift. The Mossad wasn't taking any ads or holding any press parties. *Time* also incorrectly said that Yehuda Dominitz "revealed the operation." (Not one word about the operation had appeared in the Jewish Agency official's interview with *Nekuda* magazine.)

The often unfriendly *Times* of London rhapsodized
about Israel's mission in several articles and an editorial, replete with biblical quotations. "The mod-
ern-day successors of Moses and Aaron found the
authorities in the Sudan and Ethiopia more amena-
ble than the Pharaoh was when they sought to lead
out the so-called 'lost tribe.' " The *Sunday Times* said,
"When Israel is aroused it knows no frontiers." The
BBC—in its initial reactions, anyway—and the *Daily
Express* and the *Guardian* among other British newspapers, also had words of praise. The *Scotsman* said,
"Israel extends 'a strong hand and outstretched arm'—
in the words used to describe the very first Exodus
from Egypt—to pluck her own people from the brink
of disaster." The Trotskyists were upset. And a pro-
PLO member of Parliament, Tony Marlow, said that
the Beta-Israel would be used as "front-line troops in
the conquest of the West Bank."

Radio Moscow shared Marxist Ethiopia's vision of
what had really happened: Israel had simply kidnapped non-Jewish Ethiopians and brought them to
the Jewish state against their will. A French leftist,
one Serge Thion, issued a broadside declaring that
"the Falashas are not Jewish" and that it was all part
of an Israeli plot "to grab land and massacre the Palestinian people." In Jordan, the *al-Dustur* newspaper
generously called Operation Moses "another triumph
for Zionism and Israel." But Cairo's *al-Ahram* said,
"Famine does not distinguish between Jews and non-
Jews. What Israel has done is save the Jews and leave
the non-Jews dying."

The Jewish press from Australia to France to North
America was jubilant, and for weeks, stories about the
formerly "lost Jews" filled their columns. The *Long
Island Jewish World* expressed a widespread view

when it said that "hallelujahs should be rising in the voices of the Jewish world." The London *Jewish Chronicle* said, "Once again Israel has given Jews cause for pride. The historic airlift organized to bring Ethiopian Jews to the Jewish state is a reaffirmation of the nation's dedication to the preservation of our people. . . ." In France, the *Tribune Juive* editorialized that Operation Moses had given every Jew "not only the hope but also the assurance that he is not isolated and that he can count on Israel in every situation."

In Israel, the daily *Ma'ariv* put it this way: "There was a sense of re-living days gone by, a sense of history knocking on our door." Columnist Yosef Lapid wrote, "I became a Zionist on the day I fled with my mother from the Budapest ghetto and we had nowhere to hide. They wanted to kill us and in the whole world we had no place to go. We had to return to the ghetto, but since then I have known that there has to be a place somewhere on the face of the earth which can offer haven to a Jewish child whose life is threatened by Nazis or by famine. In brief that is what Zionism is. Welcome, my black brothers. You are helping us to understand what we are doing here."

AFTER THE STORY of the airlift broke in January 1985, I was among the Western journalists who flocked to Khartoum. Most came to report on Operation Moses, as well as to continue covering the famine. Hundreds of thousands of starving refugees were flooding across Sudan's borders, and Sudan itself was hard hit by drought and food shortages.

Officials at the U.S. embassy would say nothing to reporters about any aspect of the suspended airlift.

The deputy head of mission, David Shinn, began an interview about the general refugee situation by holding his hand up in a "stop" position and saying, "Just don't ask me any questions about the Falashas, because I won't tell you anything."

Reporters were also met with silence when they questioned Sudanese officials. An ABC crew was sent out from London to visit the hundreds of Ethiopian Jews stranded in the refugee camps by the curtailed airlift. But nobody would talk to them—"We were stonewalled all the way," the team's frustrated producer told me.

During my visit to Khartoum and the camps along the Ethiopia-Sudan border, I did not disclose my interest in the Falashas for security reasons, but I was frequently asked by the educated Sudanese I met whether I had come to write about the overall refugee situation, or about the Jews. In general, the Sudanese were cynical about the airlift. A great deal of money was involved, they said, and it probably had enriched President Nimeiry, ensconced in his palace along the Blue Nile, as well as Tayeb, his security chief. They were wrong.

The only Sudanese official who would say anything at all about the airlift was a military spokesman, who stated the obvious and stopped at that: "The Arabs hate us for the Falashas." The episode clearly was providing more ammunition to powerful elements within the army and the government who were critical of Nimeiry's overall performance as head of Africa's biggest country, which had been plagued by severe economic problems, the rebellion in the south, and the famine and refugee situation. (President Nimeiry was overthrown in a military coup in

April 1985; the consensus of Sudan experts is that
Operation Moses was not a factor in his downfall.
Afterward, Sudan grew estranged from the United
States, while drawing closer to two former foes,
Ethiopia and Libya.)

Western journalists found that it was wise to avoid
too many inquiries into the status of the stranded
Ethiopian Jews. Two Canadian newsmen who were
trying to contact Falashas were detained briefly by
the Sudanese authorities. But two other journalists,
from the *New York Times* and the *Sunday Times* of
London, sidestepped the officials, flew to Gedaref, and
visited nearby Umm Rekuba, where they interviewed an Ethiopian Jew who said that some of his
children were in Israel and that he wished to join
them. This refugee was the only one who talked. The
Falashas still in Umm Rekuba, Maskar, Wad el-
Heluw, and Tuwawa had been warned not to speak
to anyone, white or black, Jew or gentile.

Aleph, who was still working out of the safe house
in Gedaref, visited the camps several times to assure
his people that the airlift would be resumed. He took
as many people out of the disease-ridden camps as
possible, bringing them to Gedaref to wait for rescue. One man named Mamu, whose wife had been put
in a separate camp when they first crossed into Sudan, had watched his father, his son, and one of his
daughters die in Umm Rekuba. Mamu and his wife
had thought each other was dead. Aleph brought them
both to Gedaref, and they met by chance in the dusty
main street of the town. "I couldn't believe my eyes,"
Mamu would recall.

The Ethiopian Jews left in the camps were more
terrified than ever of the other refugees, who contin-

ued to blame them for the famine, the pestilence, and the killing of Jesus. The Beta-Israel did not need to be reminded to keep a low profile.

THE FEW HUNDRED Jewish refugees who were stranded in Sudan after January 5 did not despair that they would be rescued. The frenzy that sometimes had overcome the Falashas earlier was no longer evident. (On one occasion during the Mossad operation in early 1984, a Western refugee official had come across a group of Beta-Israel waiting outside Gedaref for an operative who was to take them to Israel. One of the Jews, in desperation over an apparent delay, committed suicide right in front of him.)

Shortly after the story of Operation Moses hit the front pages, Washington put pressure on President Nimeiry to allow the airlift to resume. President Reagan received appeals from senators who called for the rescue of the remaining Falashas. But he had committed himself long before. Eugene Douglas, the Reagan administration's representative on refugee questions in the State Department, had been a driving force in Operation Moses, and along with the CIA and the embassy in Khartoum, he continued to keep Reagan up-to-date. (All one hundred senators signed a letter to Reagan urging resumption of the airlift. The signatures were solicited by senators Alan Cranston of California and Alphonse D'Amato of New York, who became involved through the efforts of the AAEJ and Phil Blazer, publisher of a Los Angeles newspaper called *Israel Today*. In claiming most of the credit for the resumption of the airlift, the AAEJ simply disregarded the fact that the Israeli government and the Reagan administration were already hard at work on the project. The AAEJ's statement of November 27, 1985, said that the AAEJ was "the principal catalyst for U.S. government actions" that resulted in the successful second airlift of March 1984.)

At a meeting in February with Vice President George Bush, who was preparing for a visit to Khartoum, Reagan reportedly said that he wanted the remaining Jews brought out of Sudan, regardless of the consequences, and ordered it done. Bush, a former head of the CIA, was no stranger to such requests. On the eve of his March 4 visit, Bush informed the National Press Club in Washington that among the issues he would discuss with Nimeiry was the departure of the Ethiopian Jews remaining in his country.

Nimeiry had told the *New York Times* in January that the remaining Falashas could leave Sudan at any time, as long as they did not go directly to Israel. But this was simply for public consumption and in no way reflected the actual situation. "What they tell the *Times* and what is really happening are two different matters," a State Department official commented. Nimeiry was worried about the repercussions of Operation Moses, nervous that he might be assassinated like his friend Anwar Sadat for dealing, however indirectly, with Israel. But because of his absolute dependence on American aid, Nimeiry would decide to go along. He was scheduled to pay a state visit to the United States in April and was planning to press Reagan for a promised increase in overall aid, as well as for funds that Washington had suspended because of his repressive policies and mishandling of the economy.

On March 7 Bush reached an agreement with Nimeiry for the removal of the remaining Ethiopian

Jews as soon as possible. Within a week, Washington would release about $15 million in aid to Sudan.

The White House decided that the operation was to be conducted directly by the CIA, which until then had had only a peripheral role in the rescue operations. Ambassador Hume Horan in Khartoum received a presidential order to work out the plan with the CIA station chief and to implement it within three or four days. It became immediately apparent, though, that this deadline could not be met—it would take two weeks to organize the operation.

Jerry Weaver was consulted but took no part in the planning of the new airlift, code-named Operation Sheba. But in a brief ceremony at the Khartoum embassy, Bush presented him with an award for his work in the Operation Moses airlift.

The Sudanese security forces and CIA agents spent the next few days refining the plan for Operation Sheba. The Ethiopian Jews still scattered in various camps would be gathered at an assembly point outside Tuwawa on the evening of March 21 and taken to the airstrip some eight miles outside of Gedaref, where they would spend the night. The Hercules transports would start coming in shortly before dawn.

Israeli authorities had believed that at least eleven hundred Jews were still left in the Sudanese refugee camps and in Gedaref. Some reports had put the figure as high as two thousand.

Aleph contacted the Jews in Maskar, Wad el-Heluw, and Umm Rekuba on March 20, and said, "It's time." Trucks and buses carried them to the rendezvous point outside Tuwawa, and a few hours later they were brought to the Gedaref airstrip. On March 21 an alert went out to Israeli hospitals and the corps of social workers and translators to get ready to receive "a lot of people."

The CIA operation was carried out by U.S. Air Force personnel, men and women, working in cooperation with the Israelis. All the aircraft were outfitted to seat ninety passengers each. Eighteen planes were mobilized at the U.S. Air Force base in Frankfurt, West Germany. However, at the last minute, information was received from Aleph that the number of remaining refugees was much smaller than had been reported.

Nine of the Hercules planes, crammed with food, water, and medical supplies, flew five hours from an Israeli military base outside the Red Sea port of Eilat to the dirt airstrip near the village of Showak, just outside Gedaref. Yehuda was in charge of the only Israelis on the planes—two-man teams of other veteran Ethiopian immigrants who could speak English, and four doctors. For unspecified security reasons, the Israeli Ethiopians had been instructed not to engage in conversation with the American crews, but there was inevitable banter between them. The Americans, including several blacks, were extremely curious about the African Jews.

At the Gedaref strip, which was surrounded by Sudanese secret service men, the Americans found a great deal of confusion over the whereabouts of all the refugees. It was finally determined that the number was even smaller than Aleph had thought. A duplication of names had occurred, and the lists of the people to be brought to Israel included many Ethiopians already there. Instead of eleven hundred, or two thousand, there were six hundred at the most. The American pilots also had another concern: the harmattan, a dry, dust-laden wind, had swept across the desert on the night of March 21 and threatened to disrupt the airlift. But the hot harmattan (which the Arabs consider an evil wind) died down the next morning, and the operation went off without a hitch. The CIA agents went back to the safe house in Gedaref to celebrate with champagne.

Three of the planes flew back to Israel completely empty; the food and water were left with the Sudanese authorities. The others landed at half-hour intervals outside Eilat starting at midmorning. Prime Minister Shimon Peres boarded each plane to welcome the new arrivals. The U.S. ambassador, Samuel Lewis, was there to oversee the American operation. Both men grew increasingly emotional as the refugees debarked. (In October 1985, after meeting with President Reagan, Peres told a group of American Jewish leaders, "The president was moved to tears when I thanked him for helping us [in Operation Moses].")

A total of 460 refugees were flown directly from the Gedaref airstrip to Eilat. Another 140 came out via a second route in the following days.

The mood at Eilat was euphoric in the hour before the newcomers were bused to a transit center set up near Acre in the north. A white-haired old man among the new arrivals showed Prime Minister Peres a holy book written on thick, warped lambskin, soiled with age and as wrinkled as he was. His voice cracking, the old man said: "Listen! These are the things of Moses. We have arrived!"

9

Homecoming

Operation Moses and the follow-up Operation Sheba airlifted about eight thousand Ethiopian Jews to Israel, where they joined seven thousand others who had been brought in the previous four years by the Mossad. The Jewish Agency and the government weren't prepared for the sudden influx of eight thousand—preplanning often goes by the boards in Israel—and a mad rush was on to find housing. Maintenance crews worked eighteen-hour days to prepare facilities in some sixty absorption centers and in eleven large hotels that were leased to accommodate the newcomers.

The Ethiopian immigrants were scattered all over the nation. Many were sent to the most attractive of the centers, Mevasseret Zion (Harbinger of Zion), which usually caters exclusively to Western immigrants in the professions. Israeli absorption centers serve as halfway houses to help immigrants adjust to a new language and new customs. Housing, utilities, and child care are free for six months to a year; a monthly allowance is provided for food and pocket money; and intensive Hebrew-language classes are offered. Social workers and job counselors assist new immigrants who otherwise would face a depressing bureaucratic maze out in the "real" Israel.

"We were given less than twenty-four hours' notice to be ready to receive hundreds of Ethiopians," recalls Yair Levy, the director of the Mevasseret facility, which is located six miles west of Jerusalem. Extra staff was hired and a medical clinic was set up in the center, which is built like a self-contained village, with a minimarket, school, synagogue, and nurseries. Volunteers were enlisted to help receive the newcomers and to distribute used clothing donated by hundreds of individual Israelis.

Most of the residents at the center waited for hours on a Friday afternoon in the first week of 1985 to greet the Ethiopian Jews; the observant among them saw it as their first opportunity to participate in "the ingathering of the exiles." The Ethiopian Jews finally arrived in buses from the transit center in Ashkelon. It was their third day in Israel, and many of them were still dazed. The residents, for all their good intentions, were ill-equipped to provide the Ethiopians with assistance. Many had cooked extra chicken and Sabbath delicacies, only to be told that it was too dangerous for the Ethiopians to eat such food after living on a below-subsistence diet for many months in the refugee camps of Sudan.

Residents volunteered to "adopt" Ethiopian families. Mina, a social worker at the center, said, "It's been a wonderful beginning. What remains to be seen is what will happen when the excitement wears off." But in the months after the Ethiopians had settled into the routine, a close relationship continued between them and their neighbors, many of whom had emigrated from North America, England, and South Africa.

Most of the Western immigrants living at Mevasseret had not Hebraicized their names, and many never will. But the Ethiopians, with names like Adjubu and Aloumash, were expected to do so immediately—absorption center officials felt it would help smooth their transition into Israeli society.

As has always been the case with new waves of immigrants, the children were picking up Hebrew quickly and could be heard on the playground conversing in Hebrew among themselves. The older people had the greatest difficulty with the language. It posed a major problem, and although the volunteers were happy to spend a few minutes to chat, most gave up after the perfunctory, "How are you?"

Devora and Ephraim and their four small children, who came from Ambover village, were put up in one of the identical cottages equipped with standardized Jewish Agency furniture. After six months in Israel, Ephraim, who had been a tenant farmer in Ethiopia, still didn't know what kind of work he would go into. "Anything but agriculture," he said. Devora planned to take a vocational-school course and become a seamstress.

For the first time, their marriage had experienced difficulties, primarily because the normal pattern of "father goes off to work" had been disrupted. Now, he was at home and refused to help out around the house. In Ethiopia, where Ephraim worked from dawn to sunset, it was never expected that the man of the house would help with the children or the housework. The notion that the man should do otherwise if he's not working was simply too foreign.

It had become a typical problem at Mevasseret, according to Mesved, an interpreter who lives at the center. "Many wives have complained to me that their husbands spend the afternoons and evenings with friends and refuse to assist them. I've spoken to the husbands, individually and as a group, and told them that they must help out. They nod in agreement, but go back to their old ways."

Money became another source of tension. Ephraim and Devora got a monthly allowance of about $165 to buy food and other items for their family of six. "Before the famine, we ate better in Ethiopia than we do now, because we grew all of our own food," Devora said. But the single greatest pressure on the Ethiopian families has been the worry about relatives who were left behind. Ephraim's four brothers, two sisters, and mother remain in Ambover, for example. Mesved, a former school principal who was brought to Israel in 1982, said, "I sit in my computer class trying to listen to the teacher, but my mind is in Ethiopia with my wife and daughter."

The most humiliating experience for many of the

Ethiopians has been a trip to the local grocer. After six months, they still had difficulty understanding the value of the currency (a problem shared by many others who have experienced Israel's wild inflation) and consequently often found they did not have enough money to cover all of their purchases. The cashiers would lose patience and react rudely when items had to be returned to the shelves. Courtesy is a key element in Ethiopian culture, and the new arrivals were shocked when confronted by this example of Israel's abrasive society. "The Ethiopian is very likely as bright as or brighter than the cashier, but is made to feel a fool," according to anthropologist Chaim Rosen, head of a study project on Ethiopian Jews.

Rosen, who did years of fieldwork in Ethiopia, was not surprised by the clash of Israeli and Ethiopian cultures. Well-intentioned absorption workers who were brusque, loud, or abrasive were generally unaware of how offensive they appeared to Ethiopians, who have been reared in a culture where quietness is a supreme virtue. He cited an example of ignorance about the Ethiopians: an absorption worker proudly told a reporter that at first the children were very quiet, "but now they're running around like normal kids." To the worker, "normal" meant loud. But it is repugnant in Ethiopian terms. "A parent would be most ashamed if his children became boisterous," Rosen noted. "They are trained not to raise their voices; it's a mark of nobility."

Instruction was given at Mevasseret in money management, dental hygiene, and birth control. When the Ethiopians were introduced to the Pill, it created a controversy: after a nurse presented a slide show and explained the use of the oral contraceptive, a local rabbi insisted on speaking to the Ethiopians about the importance Jewish religious law places on having children. The reaction among the Ethiopian women was mixed. Some, particularly those with eight to twelve children, were heartened by news of the Pill. Others rejected the idea. "To learn about birth control is all right," said Devora, "but to take the Pill—never!"

Mevasseret is a model absorption center and differs from the other facilities in several ways: the ratio between Ethiopian and Western immigrants allows for a personal relationship to develop between them, and most of the Western immigrants are observant Jews, who have been trying to draw the Ethiopians into mainstream religious tradition. Almost all the Ethiopian males go to the synagogue on the Sabbath, and though they don't read Hebrew, they hold a prayer book or a Bible through the service. All of the nonreading honors—such as opening the ark and rolling the Torah scroll—are given to Ethiopians. After services on Friday night and Saturday afternoon, Western immigrants accompany the Ethiopians home and help them to recite a blessing over wine. A class on the weekly Bible portion—the Torah is divided into weekly sections, and a complete reading takes one year—is given in Amharic and Hebrew every Saturday. Six hours of classes each week are devoted to practical Judaism.

Rabbi Ronald Roness, who oversees programs at absorption centers in the Jerusalem area, expressed satisfaction with the progress the Ethiopians have made and felt the religious-education program was adequate. He was upset to learn that Christian missionaries had been visiting the Ethiopian Jews at Mevasseret and elsewhere. But Mevasseret was not turning into a hotbed of discontent in the summer of 1985, as was the case with many other absorption centers. Several thousand Ethiopian Jews at various centers around the country went on strike to protest against rabbinical rulings that they must undergo ritual immersion as part of a symbolic conversion ceremony to reaffirm their Judaism. The Ethiopians at Mevasseret Zion refused to take part: "We won't be manipulated, by our people or anyone else," one of the interpreters said. By September 1985, the ritual immersion requirement would become a stormy issue among Jews in Israel and elsewhere.

THE FIFTEEN THOUSAND Ethiopian Jews now in Israel have been extremely traumatized by their experience and face some awesome social, psychological, economic, and religious problems. They also encounter a measure of racial prejudice. They have made a leap in time and space, from an Ethiopia that "slept for a thousand years, forgetful of the world" to a high-technology Israel that the world never forgets.

The only way to treat the Beta-Israel is with "respect and love," according to one Education Ministry official, a man who came to Israel from Morocco in the 1950s and does not want to see a repetition of the same mistakes that were made in the handling of North African immigrants. (The North Africans, who were sprayed with DDT upon their arrival "to kill lice," were shunted off to remote development towns or the poorest urban neighborhoods.) For the most part, the *aliyah* of the Beta-Israel engendered a national goodwill that boded well for their integration, or "absorption" as the Israelis call it. But the clouds would start forming soon enough.

One of Israel's leading anthropologists, Phyllis Palgi, head of the behavioral science department at Tel Aviv University Medical School, interviewed dozens of Ethiopian immigrants in 1984 as an adviser to the Jewish Agency. In her previous work on Moroccan Jewry, she was highly critical of the agency. But the Jewish Agency's field workers are a world apart from the retrograde bureaucratic institution, and she was impressed by their devotion and warmth toward the Beta-Israel. Hundreds of the social workers, teachers, homemaker aides, and counselors had shown a genuine identification with the immigrants and "an almost desperate search for a way to make things go right."

Palgi, who was trained by Margaret Mead, says that the Ethiopian Jews—nearly all of whom lost members of their family in Sudan or during the trek out of Ethiopia—have been through hell and therefore look at the world through fearful, untrusting eyes. For example, enormous tension exists between the Amharic-speaking Jews who come from the Gondar area and those from Tigre Province who speak Tigrean, and wild accusations have been thrown around. "This is typical of a traumatized group—they turn on each other."

But what worried Palgi most of all was the "tremendous messianic beliefs among the male Ethiopian Jews." She had come across a number of immigrants with messianic complexes, especially among the more intelligent and imaginative. They saw themselves as saviors, deluding themselves into believing that they were responsible for bringing their

people to Israel, while at the same time disparaging
the work of the real rescuers. They acted as if they
had all the answers; they became autocratic, and no
one could tell them anything. This messianic fervor,
fueled by Judaism's focus on redemption, had added
greatly to the psychological distress that Palgi dis-
cerned. It is a common phenomenon for groups who
emigrate under terrible stress, dreaming of being led
to a paradise: "It's a form of pulling yourself out of
a bad situation and toward a better life."

On the other hand, Palgi found it encouraging that
the Ethiopian Jews had organized demonstrations for
more government action in the months before Operation Moses. "It meant that they had started to become active, to take their future in their own hands
and not just accept what they are told."

Many of the immigrants know what they want and
what they don't want, and they have continued to
make their voices heard. They possess a rich and
complex culture, of which most Israelis are ignorant.
Because of their centuries-old oral tradition, their
memory skills are better developed than those of lit-
erate people, and they remember what they have
heard with faster and clearer recall. It may be true
that a good number of the Ethiopian Jews had been
unfamiliar with such things as a doorknob, running
water, electric lights, gas stoves, or telephones. But
overcoming the technological gap has been relatively simple. Dr. Steven Kaplan of Hebrew University and Dr. Rachel Tokalty of the Education Ministry
are among those who ridiculed the media's initial
emphasis on the so-called technological gap. "How
many of us understand how electrical appliances
really work?" Kaplan asks. He can cite scores of cases

in which adjustment has been inhibited more by trauma than by culture shock. Feelings of fear and bereavement are far greater impediments to integration than the technological gap.

"WE WILL MAKE many mistakes," says Uri Gordon, the head of Youth Aliyah, an organization that takes care of young immigrants who are orphans or whose parents cannot take care of them. "But criticism should take into account the massive problems we face, how different this *aliyah* is. This is a true drama here, a very complex operation that calls for wise handling."

Because of the high rate of unemployment in the outlying development towns, caused by the severe stagflation that has weakened Israel's economy, the people in some of these settlements at first expressed reluctance to have Ethiopians live among them and possibly aggravate the crisis. But in the immediate aftermath of Operation Moses, those Israelis who didn't want to receive the Ethiopian Jews were far from typical. In the Red Sea port of Eilat, for example, the mayor had been quoted as saying that the Ethiopians would not be welcomed because of the harsh economic difficulties facing the coastal city. But when the first group of newcomers arrived in Eilat, they were greeted with smiles, flowers, and a lavish feast.

The kibbutzim joined in the nationwide effort to help the newcomers, teaching Hebrew to the youngsters and offering various types of pre–military service training. The Israeli army, traditionally at the forefront in absorbing new immigrants, set up vocational guidance and special courses, and several Ethiopian Jews are now serving in the country's elite units, including the paratroopers and the Golani Brigade.

Of course there were naysayers. One editor of a sophisticated Hebrew literary review went around saying that the Ethiopian *aliyah* was a terrible disaster: "We're creating more hordes for the religious and nationalist fanatics." The editor of a government-sponsored magazine asked, "What do we need more *chak-chak'im* [slang meaning lower-class Sephardim] for?" A Moroccan-born printer said, "Give them a finger and they take an arm." An elderly German-born Jewish woman shook her head knowingly and whispered, "Just you wait." Two policemen in the Tel Aviv suburb of Petah Tikva manhandled and verbally abused three of the immigrants, saying, "Why don't you niggers go back to Africa?" Israel, it seems, has a normal percentage of racists. One fourteen-year-old new arrival told Uri Gordon, "We black Jews are very happy that there are white Jews." But unfortunately, Gordon said, the reciprocal sentiment was not universal in Israel.

Haim Aharon, chairman of the Jewish Agency's immigration department, shared the initial excitement and emotions experienced by most of the over one thousand Israelis who have been directly working with the Ethiopian immigrants. Aharon said that the main absorption goal was to protect the Ethiopians' culture, music, language, dance. "We teach them and, at the same time, encourage and want them to be independent. The veteran immigrants among them take part in our decision making. Ideally, five or six Ethiopian families in an apartment block is what we want. They have problems of leadership, and many other problems. But we'll overcome them."

He said that one of the main difficulties was the lack of a social infrastructure in the community, which makes the newcomers even more dependent on the agency and the government. Like Gordon, he felt that the battle against prejudice would become a major struggle.

Aharon and Gordon both remarked that the new immigrants learn incredibly fast and show a fierce desire for education. "They can compete with the best of Israeli youth," Gordon said. The Ethiopians were being placed in religious institutions mainly because they are traditional and wouldn't understand if Shabbat were violated, as on a secular kibbutz, he asserted. Never more than 30 percent of the pupils in an institution are Ethiopians. "In these institutions, some of the newcomers are already rising to the top."

THE RABBINICAL DEMANDS on the Beta-Israel, and the Ethiopians' adamant refusal to undergo any ritual ceremony, set the immigrants at loggerheads with the Chief Rabbinate, which administers matters of life, death, and marriage in a country where church and state remain unseparated.

Several prominent rabbis were split over the immersion requirement in the months following Operation Moses, and bitter charges were exchanged between religious leaders. Until November 1984, the rabbis had required that a drop of blood be drawn from the penis of Ethiopian males to ensure their Jewishness, but the Chief Rabbinate then decided that the immersion-in-water ceremony would be enough. Males were still checked to see if they were properly circumcised.

"It's not just the so-called militants who have re-

fused to go through these ceremonies," according to
Shoshana Ben-Dor of Jerusalem's Ben-Zvi Institute.
Ben-Dor, a former activist on behalf of the Ethiopian
Jews who has become an expert on the Beta-Israel's
religious practices, said that "a good many Ethiopians have refused to go through any ceremony on
purely religious grounds, maintaining that they are
already Jews." One Ethiopian representative told
Prime Minister Peres that his people had left the land
of Israel thousands of years ago carrying the Bible and
that they had returned still carrying it. Yet the Chief
Rabbinate wanted to "take away our Jewishness" by
forcing them to undergo the "degrading" ritual immersion in order to become "complete Jews." The
immersion requirement recalled Christian baptism
and was anathema to the Beta-Israel.

The *giur l-chumra,* or conversion due to doubt, was
first applied to the Falashas by former chief Sephardi rabbi Ovadia Yosef, the man who, in 1973, did
the most to push for recognition of the Beta-Israel as
Jews, ruling that they were the Lost Tribe of Dan. But
in 1985, Yosef, who had become the spiritual leader
of the Sephardi ultra-Orthodox Shas political party,
changed his mind about conversion. He said that after
studying the Beta-Israel's religious practices, he had
come to believe that no ceremony whatsoever was
necessary.

Rabbi Israel Lau of Netanya, a well-known Ashkenazic religious leader, and Rabbi David Chelouche
of Netanya, a Sephardi who is a member of the Rabbinical Council, supported Ovadia Yosef's stand.
Chelouche performed a wedding of Ethiopian Jews
without asking to see their identity cards (the new
immigrants all get an identity number but do not get

the identity *cards* until they've gone through the conversion ceremony). Support also came from former chief Ashkenazic rabbi Shlomo Goren. But the majority of the nation's religious leaders backed the rabbinate, while saying that the Jewishness of the Beta-Israel community had been firmly established in matters such as prayer service and burial. But for marriage, they still insisted on immersion, to prevent possible mixed marriage. Many of the nation's leading religious figures issued a statement in September 1985 declaring that "the serious fear has arisen that some intermingling with non-Jews may have occurred in the course of time and that no legal conversion may have taken place." They felt the Ethiopian Jews should go through the act of renewal of the covenant, "in accordance with established practice for some time now concerning immigrants from whatever land, in cases where similar doubt has arisen." Only thus could the Jewish law be upheld.

Dissenters from within the religious community called this double-talk, citing the fact that the Jews of India—called B'nei Israel—had run into the same kind of trouble when they immigrated to Israel a generation earlier. (The rabbinical authorities initially blocked their marriages, asserting that obvious intermarriage had occurred in India. The Indian Jews eventually forced the rabbis to remove the obstacles by staging demonstrations and hunger strikes.) But the great majority of the religious community stood behind the Chief Rabbinate. State-supported schools run by the Habad sect said that they wouldn't allow Ethiopian students to continue their education unless they went through the conversion ceremony.

The Ethiopian community itself has been divided

over the issue: although almost all are opposed to the ceremony, sharp differences have emerged over what course to follow. Some of the new immigrants were threatened with violence by young Ethiopian activists if they went through with the ceremony. An alleged "hit list" was drawn up by a small radical group of Ethiopians, who talked about killing the chief rabbis and those who support them on the issue.

The protesters, especially the younger generation, were attacking what they called an insulting decision that raises questions about whether or not they are really Jews. "We have enough prejudice to contend with," one Beta-Israel high school student said on a television program for youth. "Children are often cruel to each other as is. Some kids don't like the color of our skin. The rabbis don't help matters by questioning our Jewishness." A possible outcome is that many of the Beta-Israel will become secular. Shoshana Ben-Dor cites the example of one young man who was studying to be a rabbi: "As soon as they subjected him to the conversion ceremony, he took off his yarmulke."

Rabbi Menachem Waldman of Nir Etzion, who is compiling a history of rabbinical attitudes toward the Beta-Israel, remarked that although he may not have liked the bluntness of the Habad sect's rejection of Ethiopian pupils in their schools, he understood it. (A secret government report said that Waldman, at one time the rabbinate's point man with the Ethiopians, was one of the names on the alleged hit-list.) Waldman maintained that "according to Halacha [Jewish law], the Ethiopian Jews must go through the immersion ceremony. That's that. That was the decision of the two chief rabbis and the Rabbinical

Council in November 1984. The only dissenter was Rabbi Chelouche. There is no chance that the rabbinate will just cave in to demands to dispense with the conversion ceremony."

Another defender of the rabbinate asserted that most of the Beta-Israel religious leaders—the seventeen Ethiopian *kesim* (priests) who were in Israel when the airlift ended—were in favor of the conversion ceremony. They regarded it as a bridge to their adaptation to "modern" Judaism—that is, the two-thousand-year-old rabbinical tradition, which they did not have. But Rabbi Yosef Adane, son of a well-known *kes* and the first Ethiopian Jew to become a rabbi, said that the great majority of the community remains virulently opposed to the ritual. "Some of the *kesim* who already went through the ceremony don't really care, and a smaller number refuse outright. But the majority is against." This was especially true of the Jews brought out during Operation Moses. However, they were split over methods, with only four *kesim* actually lining up with the militants.

Adane himself has been in a delicate position—it was hard for him to talk against the rabbinate—but he said of the Beta-Israel dissenters, "It is their privilege to say no after fighting for their Judaism for thousands of years." He agreed with the pronouncements of Rabbi Ovadia Yosef that the conversion ceremony had become absolutely unnecessary. "The whole issue can cause great damage to the community because of the militancy that it awakens," he said. "Already we're seeing great resistance to going along with Talmudic dietary laws, which we did not practice in Ethiopia."

In July 1985, Prime Minister Peres held a series of

meetings with the chief rabbis and with representatives of the Beta-Israel community and worked out a
formula to get around the impasse over immersion.
But the agreement, under which the rabbinical courts
would determine the personal status of Ethiopian
Jews applying to be married, did not hold—the chief
rabbis backed out. Nor were the Ethiopian immigrants easy to negotiate with: lacking expertise in
Halacha and inexperienced in the ways of their new
country, they often changed their minds and broached
fresh, unreasonable demands just as the rabbis indicated some willingness to come to terms. Peres said
the dispute should be viewed as "a family spat" and
that "only distance and time, not religion, separated
us in the past." The Ethiopians told Peres that they
were deeply sorry that publicity about the community's opposition to immersion was being used against
Israel. "We didn't want the whole world to know
about it," one of the representatives said.

The debate over conversion reflected some of the
deep splits among Jews in Israel and elsewhere. The
secular Citizens Rights party said Peres should not
have gone to the chief rabbis to plead for the Ethiopians. By doing so, he was "relinquishing the government's legal authority" and making the Orthodox
rabbis the sole judge of "who's a Jew and who's a half
Jew." Other anticlerical groups joined in the fray, including the leftist Mapam and centrist Shinui parties. They claimed "solidarity" with the Ethiopian
demonstrators. In New York, Rabbi Alexander
Schindler, leader of the Reform movement, condemned the rabbinical authorities for insisting on
ritual conversion. The right-wing Tehiya party was
split between Knesset member Geula Cohen, who

described the Chief Rabbinate as "cruel," and her colleague Rabbi Eliezer Waldman, who defended the chief rabbis. Geula Cohen's brother, a prominent religious figure, sided with the chief rabbis. Yuval Ne'eman, the head of the Tehiya party, said that the Beta-Israel should go back to Ethiopia if they were so dissatisfied. One important rabbi, She'ar Yishuv Hacohen, suggested that the Ethiopians be regarded as a separate community, like the Karaites or Samaritans (Jewish sects that do not have the rabbinical tradition), if they continued to defy the rabbinate. But most rabbis have agreed that the Ethiopians will be considered a full-fledged Jewish community.

In late summer 1985, hundreds of Ethiopian Jews intensified their struggle by staging a sit-in across the street from the Chief Rabbinate in Jerusalem. For weeks, they camped out in front of the luxurious Plaza Hotel, attracting growing support from secular Israelis and liberal politicians who saw an opportunity to strike a blow at the rabbinate. The demonstrators brought their wives and children, who were pulled out of schools and absorption centers. They felt their dignity as a community was threatened. But after a few weeks, the demonstration itself became a demeaning spectacle. The chief rabbis, anxious to preserve the Halacha, felt they could go no further in yielding ground. Both sides soon boxed themselves in. The media, with the exception of the religious newspapers, went overboard in lining up with the Ethiopians—the result not of genuine concern for the Ethiopians but of the continuing *Kulturkampf* between the secular and religious populations. A group of leading artists and intellectuals issued a statement saying, "We hang our heads in shame at the plight of our brethren, emigrants from Ethiopia. Saving this remnant of Jewry, bringing it to Israel, and its absorption in the country were meant to be the most clear-cut proof of the multifaceted aspects of the Jewish people and the clearest denial of the alleged racism inherent in ourselves and in our national, religious heritage. This magnificent Zionist endeavor has now been besmirched." Although the papers reported growing sympathy for the protesters, a backlash was building up. When one of the leaders of the demonstration said that the Ethiopians wouldn't have come to Israel if they had known their Jewishness would be questioned, the reaction on the street was "So let them go back."

Fears arose that the young militants might resort to violence or suicide. But some observers saw a potentially positive side to the struggle over the immersion issue, saying that in a perverse way, the difficulties with the rabbinate were also accelerating the Ethiopians' absorption into Israeli society. "They are learning the ropes," one newspaper commented, "the uses of politics, demonstrations, the law and the media. They are also learning that they are not alone, that a large sector of the population sympathizes with their plight." Most of the Ethiopian Jews who had been deeply involved in Operation Moses and in the earlier efforts to gain recognition of their people's rights as Jews, including Yehuda and Aleph, were wary of the demonstration or altogether opposed, on the grounds that it was alienating not only much of the religious community but many other Israelis as well, and that it was causing severe social damage to the community. Yona Bogala also expressed his opposition to the demonstration. But their voices generally went unheeded by the new immigrants.

The strike finally ended in late September, after a compromise formula was worked out by Prime Minister Peres. The agreement involved a letter from Peres to the Ethiopian community and another letter from the chief rabbis to the prime minister. Under the formula, members of the community wishing to be married must apply to their local rabbinical marriage registrar, who will examine their personal status "according to our holy Torah." One of the young leaders of the demonstration, Adiso Masala, said, "We have decided to put our trust in the chief rabbis and to see how they carry out the agreement." But within weeks the agreement broke down, and the two sides were once again at loggerheads.

THE BETA-ISRAEL community is not homogeneous. Of the pioneer group of about 150 Ethiopian Jews who came to Israel years ago, most have ceased to be religious. Many Ethiopian Jews who lived in the big town of Gondar or in Addis Ababa are also less likely to be observant. Anthropologist Chaim Rosen feels it is a great distortion to portray all Ethiopians as being scrupulously observant of ritual, and speculates that this image was pushed by people who were interested in arousing sympathy for the rescue cause.

But for the most part, the Beta-Israel have remained a religion-oriented community. Initially, they were shocked by the lack of observance in Israel, and crushed when told by religious teachers that their observances were all wrong, that they were not "really" religious. The new immigrants wanted their children to be educated in religious schools, but, in Shoshana Ben-Dor's opinion, it was a terrible thing to force the Ethiopians into the frameworks of the Habad or Aguda ultra-Orthodox institutions. "It's not healthy for them," she said. "They need a broad education. Not everything should be connected to the Torah."

She told of a brilliant nine-year-old girl who had attended a Habad school for two years. "She gets top marks, but learns only about religious subjects and is not taught how to think." Practices that limit intellectual development are reinforced in Israel; for instance, religious education places extreme emphasis on rote learning. "It's a shame," Ben-Dor said, "because we know that we're dealing with a group that as a whole has tremendous intellectual potential."

A possible alternative that has been suggested by several education experts and social workers is to set up special institutions that divide education into three parts: standard schooling, religious instruction, and vocational training. In 1985, the Education Ministry sought $10 million from a reluctant Treasury to hire more teachers and find classrooms for thousands of Ethiopian children. It also announced a new program for teaching the immigrants "contemporary Judaism as practiced in Israel."

Nine months after Operation Moses, even during the long strike against the rabbinate, most of the immigrants were still attending Hebrew classes in the mornings. But they were left with nothing to do for the rest of the day. One outspoken government worker—Rina, Yehuda's wife—was highly critical of the government for failing to come up with a comprehensive absorption plan. "The immigrants are being victimized by competing agencies and vested interests who haven't got a clue about what to do. It's nothing but chaos out there." Even months after arrival, some people had not yet been reunited with their families. "The immigrants are left confused. What we have here is a real social disaster in the making."

An immediate problem was to find permanent housing for the three thousand new arrivals who had been given temporary lodging in hotels. "These people with their dignified culture, their respect for elders, were crammed into 'four-star' nightmares for many months after they were rescued," said Rina. "They couldn't even give a guest a cup of coffee—the drinking of coffee is a very important social ritual. The kids instantly learned that their fathers were no longer breadwinners and that their mothers no longer prepared food and took care of their clothing and housing. It caused great damage. They were left for most of the day with nothing to do. It would have been much better to put them in tents, in *ma'aborot* [the temporary housing built for immigrants in the 1950s]. It would have preserved instead of broken down the family structure." But by the end of their first summer in Israel, these Ethiopians finally started to get permanent housing.

Serious problems developed in most absorption centers as well. Some Ethiopian Jews had lived at the centers for more than three years. The government was not moving fast enough. There was a lack of centers like Mevasseret Zion, or Michmoret near Netanya, where the immigrants live in separate dwellings, in an atmosphere that recalls the freedom of their village life.

A central coordinating body with the authority to cut through red tape might have been able to overcome petty rivalries between agencies and begin to deal with the housing situation. But in the months following the airlift, too many agencies continued to be involved, and this led to broken promises and unnecessary confusion.

Although top government and Jewish Agency officials have said repeatedly that they are sensitive to the feelings and needs of the Ethiopian Jews, some of them have shown a certain callousness. For example, the Jewish Agency authorized the Jewish National Fund to bring six busloads of American tourists to snap pictures of the Ethiopians at the Gilo absorption center in Jerusalem. The immigrants didn't know who these people were. No one explained to them why they were being taken out of their Hebrew classes to be photographed. "It is a way to raise money. What it did was to cause bruised feelings and a week-long strike," according to one worker. The agency, which runs all the absorption centers, has also allowed a tourism company to bring smaller groups to visit the Ethiopians.

The Jewish Agency does not enjoy wide respect among the Ethiopian community, which recalls that the organization followed and never led on the question of Ethiopian Jews, and that the leaks that stymied Operation Moses started with Chairman Arye Dulzin. The mishandling of important aspects of absorption deepened the distrust. In recent years many voices in Israel have said that the agency should be disbanded and that the work of integrating new immigrants from around the world should be reorganized and put exclusively in the hands of the government ministries.

The Absorption Ministry's committee on Ethiopian Jewry kept in constant touch with the veteran immigrants, who were given an important role in decision making. But in the continuing war between the agency and the ministry, knowledgeable agency field-workers say that the ministry "has no specially trained personnel for this; they never did it right and still don't. They believe everybody is an ingrate." Furthermore, in an emergency situation it took the Absorption Ministry ten months to come up with a long-range plan for the integration of the Ethiopian immigrants.

The ardor of a few of the Israeli workers who initially showed great enthusiasm toward the emigrants from Africa cooled when they realized that they were dealing with grown-up people who had demands and minds of their own. Five hundred Ethiopian immigrants demonstrated in March 1985 against what they said was the patronizing attitude of some of the people who work with them on a daily basis. They called for permanent housing as soon as possible and said that they wanted to live in urban centers and not in decaying development towns. They rejected agricultural settlements, declaring, "We'll be farmers no more."

THE BETA-ISRAEL, a dexterous people who are used to a very full workday, have been upset about being kept idle for months on end. They want and need employment commensurate with their learning. The crafts that many of them practiced in Ethiopia, such as metalworking, pottery making, and weaving, put them near the bottom of the social ladder in the Amhara-dominated society; and they have not been eager to resume these crafts in Israel. But in Western society handcrafted goods are much in demand, and a weaver or a potter is admired, not looked down upon. The employment opportunity is clear.

At Mevasseret Zion, textile artist Susan Hazan teaches commercial weaving methods to Ethiopians who have rare handcrafting skills. In the Galilee city of Safad, where thirty-five local families have formed a hospitality committee for the new immigrants, potter Daniel Flatauer has set up a ceramics shop with the Ethiopians. Funding came from the American Association for Ethiopian Jewry. The hospitality committee, organized by Yehoshua Sivan, has been active in both religious and vocational education, as well as in bringing the newcomers into local homes.

Safad social worker David Bedein has been trying to organize an Ethiopian cottage industry for export, concentrating on carpentry. Bedein, who is among those who believe that the new immigrants need a combined vocational, religious, and secular education, helped persuade several carpenters to take Ethiopian apprentices. He commented that the community as a whole has been highly supportive of the new immigrants and that Safad mayor Zev Pearl believes the newcomers will help attract investment in the town.

Across the street from Safad city hall is Beit Busal, one of the town's three absorption centers filled to capacity with Ethiopian immigrants. Yaffa, a Hebrew teacher at the center, said that her students are eager for knowledge and are highly motivated. In the week before Passover 1985, her students, who had been in Israel anywhere from three to seven months, learned the Hebrew words associated with the story of the festival that is the most meaningful to Ethiopian Jews. Many of the young people at the Safad center described in halting Hebrew how sorry they were that their parents, or siblings, had died before they too could celebrate Passover in the Holy Land.

At the Yemin Orde Youth Village, a center seventy miles to the west, high up on Mount Carmel and overlooking the Mediterranean, one hundred Ethiopian youngsters live and study. Many of them had been separated from their parents in the refugee camps of Sudan. Months after the last of the Ethiopian Jews in Sudan were airlifted from Khartoum and Gedaref, it had finally become clear that about one-quarter of these children were orphans. At one point, the despondency of the children prompted the staff to set up a "Group of Hope," which drew up lists giving the names, descriptions, and last-known whereabouts of missing relatives; these lists were to be passed on to the Jewish Agency.

The director of the youth village, Dr. Chaim Peri, and his staff employed unconventional methods to bridge gaps in communication and understanding between the Ethiopians and youths from sixteen other countries. For several weeks, the staff allowed a lamb to roam free. The children soon "adopted" the lamb, feeding it and taking it for walks. Then Dr. Peri suggested that the lamb be sacrificed in keeping with the Ethiopian Jewish custom marking the first day of the Passover month of Nisan—but only if the majority of all the youngsters at the institution approved. He suggested that the matter be put to a vote.

The youngsters were encouraged to set up "political parties" that were for or against the slaughter, and the ensuing campaign was a spirited one. The Ethiopian youths were almost evenly divided, but the majority of the other children voted to spare the lamb.

The object of the exercise was both to test the attitude of the Beta-Israel youths after they had been exposed to Western influences and to demonstrate the importance of the democratic process.

Several graduates of the youth village are now serving in the Israel Defense Forces. Another has been accepted to the Technion, the Israeli MIT. Dr. Peri's aim was not merely to educate the youngsters and acquaint them with the various facets of Israeli society but also "to raise the level of their aspirations. . . . If people see an Ethiopian immigrant in one of the elite units like the paratroopers regiment, it reflects credit not just on him but on the whole community."

One of the youngsters, Ya'acov, told a reporter of the initial problems of integrating into Israeli society: "We didn't know how to behave toward the other children nor they to us, and sometimes fights started. Slowly we learned how to deal with each other, and now everything is fine."

According to a poll conducted for Youth Aliyah a few months after Operation Moses, over 90 percent of the young Ethiopian immigrants were happy in their new homes. Most of the teenagers felt they were treated as equal citizens, while only about a tenth felt they were not equal. Some complained that "Israelis want blacks only to play basketball" (Israel's national league basketball teams include many American blacks, some of whom were accorded "instant" conversions to Judaism). The things that bothered them the most were Sabbath desecration, lack of respect for religion, bad manners and intolerance, and denigration of Israeli leaders, parents, and teachers. They were most enthusiastic about seeing a "Jewish

army" and a "Jewish police force." They were also
pleased by the abundance of food and by the enthusiasm of their teachers. One out of ten had met with
hostility or insulting jokes.

SOME THREE HUNDRED Ethiopian Jews live in the Jewish settlement of Kiryat Arba, next to the large West
Bank town of Hebron, and have been received with
open arms. Most of the people of Kiryat Arba are religious nationalists, opposed to giving up an inch of
any part of the Promised Land. Although there is a
considerable amount of patronizing toward the Beta-
Israel by these passionate patriots, the warmth of their
reception cannot be denied. Behind it all lies a shared
vision of redemption. The religious nationalists believe it is vital to swell Jewish settlement in the territories, and they see some of the added numbers in
the Beta-Israel, who have been "miraculously redeemed" perhaps for this very purpose. (A significant number of the new arrivals have become
supporters of the extremist politician Meir Kahane.)

The United States has officially asked Israel not to
settle Ethiopian Jews in the disputed territories.
Washington has said that it would cut off some $15
million in aid for the absorption of the Beta-Israel if
they are settled on the West Bank or in Gaza. The Israeli government assured the United States that the
Ethiopians would not be sent to live in the territories. In May 1985 Gush Emunim (Bloc of the Faith-
ful, the driving force of the settler movement) held a
major demonstration in Jerusalem to protest against
the U.S. policy. Hundreds of Ethiopian Jews, wearing the knitted yarmulkes that have become the
trademark of the mystical-nationalist movement, took

part in the protest. The Beta-Israel had become pawns in the game of "redemption politics."

THE DIVISIONS AMONG the Ethiopian Jews could hamper their resettlement, according to Rahamim Elazar, a veteran Ethiopian immigrant who is connected to the National Council for Ethiopian Jews. The council, headed by Yael Rom of Haifa, is one of several "mixed" groups. In addition, there are also a bewildering number of exclusively Ethiopian organizations—the "Ramat Gan group," for example, the Israel Association of Ethiopian Immigrants, and others.

The various groups recognize in principle the need for a centralized leadership, but in practice they continue to go their own ways; and the new immigrants are left confused about whom to believe. This is all very much in the Israeli tradition. It was also impossible to unite Russian immigrant groups. A handful of the *kesim*, along with some of the more radical activists, have put in their bid as the leaders of the community. In reaction, another, informal, group has emerged, composed of the most prominent veteran immigrants, including those who led the Zionist movement in Ethiopia and who took part in the actual rescue in Sudan; this is undoubtedly a very positive development. Among the Beta-Israel in Ethiopia, Yona Bogala was respected because of his education and position, and he wielded power because of his position as paymaster, the funnel for Jewish funds to his people. But neither he nor the priests were true political leaders.

Although Yona Bogala remains a venerated figure among many in the community, after he came out in opposition to the sit-in demonstration across from the rabbinate, some of the militants and their supporters dismissed him as an Uncle Tom. Since 1979 he has lived in semiretirement in a modest housing project in Petah Tikva, near Tel Aviv. "It's up to the young people now," he told me shortly after Operation Moses was completed. Despite his frail health, Yona in his late seventies continues to work, doing translations and writing for the Absorption Ministry's new Amharic newspaper. There is also a possibility that a two-volume Hebrew-Amharic dictionary that he worked on for many years will finally be published. Yona has been an educator for over fifty years and believes that the key to the integration of Ethiopian Jews in Israel lies in learning. "We're here, thanks to God. Now it's up to the people of Israel to help our people with what we lack—education. It's not an easy task, but I believe it will be done."

He does not think that a "color problem" will emerge in Israel, despite some ugly incidents. Commenting on one occurrence, in which a group of Hasidic Jews refused to allow several Ethiopian Jewish youths to pray at the Western Wall, Yona said, "How horrible they are to do this—to hurt our hearts, to injure our people. Do these people really believe that they're following the *mitzvoth* [the 613 holy imperatives]?"

Yona wears a yarmulke, which he never did in Ethiopia. "I believe, and always have, in the Torah and the prophets. It speaks great things to me that the Jews of Ethiopia are now here. It was written that there will come a time when Jews from the four corners of the earth will come back to the Holy Land. It may take many more generations, but there's no doubt

in my mind that the process of redemption has begun. It is the beginning of the time of the Messiah."

The torment of separation that affects almost every
family of Ethiopian Jews in Israel was also felt by
Yona Bogala. His wife was forced to return to Addis
Ababa from Israel in 1984. The Ethiopian authorities
had allowed her out for only a few months, and relatives, including Yona's brother who lives in the
Ethiopian capital, had signed a document guaran-
teeing her return. If she refused to come back, the
relatives would face imprisonment. One of Yona's
daughters was in Addis with her mother. His six sons
are all in Israel: two of them are employed by banks,
two are working at absorption centers with the newcomers, one works for Israel Aircraft Industries, and
the youngest is a kibbutznik. Another daughter was
studying in Montreal.

Despite all that his people have suffered, Yona feels
that "it is a miracle we have been saved. In my last
years in Ethiopia, I thought our tribe was lost, without hope for *aliyah*. Everything—our schools, the aid
projects—everything seemed in vain. Every day, our
tribe was being reduced, as youths left the villages
and tradition broke down. Life in Ethiopia was a
punishment. Even our liturgical language, Ge'ez, was
a punishment; we had to adopt it because we had lost
Hebrew. But suddenly, we have Hebrew again. *That*
is our tradition."

They are at home. For most of the Ethiopian Jews
who have been in Israel for some years, it was a long,
painful struggle in an Israel that wasn't then open to
the Ethiopian Jews the way it is now. Yehuda, who
had first seen Israel as a child and who twenty-five
years later performed heroically for his people, put it

this way: "We can teach our people a great deal, spare them a lot of the pain that we suffered trying to win acceptance in Israeli society. And it's a different Israel now, as far as we're concerned. The attitude toward us is much more positive. We are survivors."

Selected Bibliography

Aescoly, A. Z. "The Falashas: A Bibliography." *Kiryat Sepher* 12 (1935–36): 254–65, 370–83, 498–505; 13 (1936–37): 250–65, 383–93, 506.

Ashkenazi, Michael, and Alex Weingrad. *Ethiopian Immigrants in Beersheba: An Anthropological Study of the Absorption Process.* Highland Park, Ill.: American Association for Ethiopian Jews, 1984.

Faitlovitch, Jacques. "The Falashas." In *American Jewish Year Book: 5681*, 80–110. Philadelphia: Jewish Publication Society of America, 1920.

Hess, Robert L. "An Outline of Falasha History." In

Proceedings of the Third International Conference of Ethiopian Studies, 99–112. Addis Ababa: Institute of Ethiopian Studies, 1969.

Kahana, Yael. *Among Long Lost Brothers* (in Hebrew). Tel Aviv: Am Oved, 1977.

Kessler, David. *The Falashas: The Forgotten Jews of Ethiopia*. London: George Allen and Unwin, 1982.

Leslau, Wolf. "The Black Jews of Ethiopia." *Commentary* 7 (1949): 216–24.

———, ed. and trans. *Falasha Anthology*. New Haven: Yale University Press, 1951.

Messing, Simon. *The Story of the Falashas: "Black Jews" of Ethiopia*. Brooklyn, N.Y.: Balshon Printing Co., 1982.

Parfitt, Tudor. *Operation Moses*. London: George Weidenfeld and Nicolson, 1985.

Quirin, James. "The Beta-Israel (Falasha) in Ethiopian History: Caste Formation and Culture Change." Ph.D. diss., University of Michigan, 1977.

Rapoport, Louis. *The Lost Jews: Last of the Ethiopian Falashas*. New York: Stein and Day, 1980.

Schoenberger, Michelle. "The Falashas of Ethiopia: An Ethnographic Study." Ph.D. diss., Cambridge University, 1975.

Sergew Hable Selassie. *Ancient and Medieval Ethiopian History to 1270*. Addis Ababa: United Printers, 1972.

Stern, Henry Aaron. *Wanderings among the Falashas in Abyssinia, 1862*. London: Frank Cass and Co., 1968.

Taddesse, Tamrat. *Church and State in Ethiopia, 1270–1527*. Oxford: Oxford University Press, 1972.

Ullendorff, Edward. *Ethiopia and the Bible*. Oxford: Oxford University Press, 1968.

Index *

226

INDEX